Poverty and Children's Adjustment

Suniya S. Luthar

Volume 41
Developmental Clinical Psychology and Psychiatry

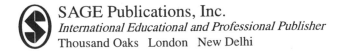

SAGE Publications, Inc.
International Educational and Professional Publisher
Thousand Oaks   London   New Delhi

For information:

SAGE Publications, Inc.
2455 Teller Road
Thousand Oaks, California 91320
E-mail: order@sagepub.com

SAGE Publications Ltd.
6 Bonhill Street
London EC2A 4PU
United Kingdom

SAGE Publications India Pvt. Ltd.
M-32 Market
Greater Kailash I
New Delhi 110 048 India

Printed in the United States of America

Library of Congress Cataloging-in-Publication Data

Luthar, Suniya S.
    Poverty and children's adjustment / by Suniya S. Luthar.
        p. cm.—(Developmental clinical psychology and psychiatry series; v. 41)
    Includes bibliographical references (p.) and index.
    ISBN 0-7619-0518-9 (cloth: acid-free paper)
    ISBN 0-7619-0519-7 (pbk.: acid-free paper)
    1. Poor children—United States—Psychology. 2. Socially handicapped children—United States—Psychology. 3. Poverty—United States—Psychological aspects. 4. Adjustment (Psychology) in children—United States. 5. Child psychopathology—United States. I. Title.
    II. Series: Developmental clinical psychology and psychiatry; v. 41.
    HV741 .L88 1999
    362.7'086'9420973—dc21   98-51240

This book is printed on acid-free paper.

99 00 01 02 03 04 05 7 6 5 4 3 2 1

Acquisition Editor:	Jim Nageotte
Editorial Assistant:	Heidi Van Middlesworth
Production Editor:	Denise Santoyo
Editorial Assistant:	Nevair Kabakian
Typesetter:	Lynn Miyata
Cover Designer:	Candice Harman
Indexer:	Virgil Diodato

For my mother, Naresh Luthar,
who has made so much possible.

CONTENTS

SERIES EDITOR'S INTRODUCTION

Interest in child development and adjustment is by no means new. Yet, only recently has the study of children benefited from advances in both clinical and scientific research. Advances in the social and biological sciences, the emergence of disciplines and subdisciplines that focus exclusively on childhood and adolescence, and greater appreciation of the impact of such influences as the family, peers, and school have helped accelerate research on developmental psychopathology. Apart from interest in the study of child development and adjustment for its own sake, the need to address clinical problems of adulthood naturally draws one to investigate precursors in childhood and adolescence.

Within a relatively brief period, the study of psychopathology among children and adolescents has proliferated considerably. Several different professional journals, annual book series, and handbooks devoted entirely to the study of children and adolescents and their adjustment document the proliferation of work in the field. Nevertheless, there is a paucity of resource material that presents information in an authoritative, systematic, and disseminable fashion. There is a need within the field to convey the latest developments and to represent different disciplines, approaches, and conceptual views to the topics of childhood and adolescent adjustment and maladjustment.

The Sage Series on Developmental Clinical Psychology and Psychiatry is designed to uniquely serve several needs of the field. The Series encompasses individual monographs prepared by experts in the fields of clinical child psychology, child psychiatry, child development, and related disciplines. The primary focus is on developmental psychopathology which refers broadly here to the diagnosis, assessment, treatment, and prevention of problems that arise in the period from infancy through adolescence. A working assumption of the Series is that understanding, identifying, and treating problems of youth must draw on multiple disciplines and diverse views within a given discipline.

The task for individual contributors is to present the latest theory and research on various topics including specific types of dysfunction, diagnostic and treatment approaches, and special problem areas that affect adjustment. Core topics within clinical work are addressed by the Series. Authors are asked to bridge potential theory, research and clinical practice, and to outline the current status and future directions. The goals of the Series and the tasks presented to individual contributors are demanding. We have been extremely fortunate in recruiting leaders in the fields who have been able to translate their recognized scholarship and expertise into highly readable works on contemporary topics.

In this book, Dr. Suniya Luthar examines *Poverty and Children's Adjustment.* The broad and pervasive impact of poverty on children's mental and physical health and adjustment are well-known. Dr. Luthar focuses on processes that exacerbate or ameliorate the effects on personal, emotional, and social development of the child. Among the many features that make this book unique is the focus on the moderators and mediators of poverty. *Moderators,* that is those factors that influence the impact of poverty, and *mediators,* the processes and mechanisms through which poverty influence child adjustment, lead to a meticulous evaluation of several topics critical to understanding child development. Examples include how poverty is influenced by characteristics of the child (e.g., intelligence, temperament), parents (e.g., parent psychopathology, teen pregnancy), family (e.g., marital relations, presence of extended family members), peer relations, schools, and neighborhoods, to mention a few of the topics. The book presents a sophisticated view of influences by emphasizing how the effects of risk and protective factors are modified by other influences such as ethnicity, child age and stage of development, and contexts and how influences can be reciprocal, bidirectional, and cumulative. The impact of poverty is enormous, as we are shown in this book. The global nature of the construct and the dependence on complex forces (e.g., education, economics) not easily harnessed can make conceptualization, research, and intervention daunting. Dr. Luthar conveys many specific mechanisms and processes through which the influences of poverty operate and hence provides multiple leads for advancing research and for intervening to help children. Her in-depth knowledge of key issues, current research, and theory, as well as her own program of research on risk and protective factors of children and adolescents, provide the basis for an authoritative, comprehensive, and cohesive presentation. The book is quite extraordinary in its contribution to understanding poverty and advancing prospects for improving child adjustment.

ALAN E. KAZDIN, PHD
Series Editor

PREFACE

The focus of this book is on risk and protective processes that modify the effects of poverty on children's social and emotional adjustment. The attempt is to integrate findings of empirical research conducted over the past three decades, on processes implicated in the adjustment of children facing socioeconomic deprivation. The bulk of the research presented here derives from developmental psychology, a discipline which accords much emphasis to elucidating the *psychological processes* that underlie effects of "social address" variables, such as socioeconomic status, on child development (Bronfenbrenner, 1986; Zigler, Lamb, & Child, 1982). In addition, this review draws upon empirical evidence from several other disciplines concerned with children in poverty, including anthropology, sociology, epidemiology, pediatrics, psychiatry, and social work.

I am deeply grateful to Alan Kazdin for the invitation to write this book, as well as for his unfailing good humor throughout the process. My special thanks to Herbert Ginsburg and Jacob Burack for their substantive comments on previous drafts, and to my students Bronwyn Becker and Shawn Latendresse for their many contributions to this effort.

For diverse forms of support of my work, all critical, I am indebted to my mentors Edward Zigler and S. Anandalakshmy; to colleagues at Teachers College, Columbia University, the Yale Substance Abuse Center, and the APT Foundation, New Haven; and to the National Institute on Drug Abuse (grants RO1-11498, RO1-10726, P50-09241, K21-00202), the Social Sciences Research Council, and the William T. Grant Foundation. For their moral support over time and particularly through the preparation of this book, I am very grateful to my family: the late Mr. L. N. Suri, Anju Seth, Karuna Kumar, Judith Benenson, and especially my husband, Shiv, and children, Nikhil and Nina Kumar.

Finally, I owe a great deal to collaborators in Connecticut—Andrew Karchich, Richard Mayer, George Moran, and Joyce Undella—who made it possible for me to begin, and later continue, my research on resilience and vulnerability among urban high school students. And for the many invaluable insights provided and lessons taught, my heartfelt appreciation goes to the children and families who have generously joined me in my research efforts over the years.

Suniya S. Luthar

1

INTRODUCTION

Some reservation families are so poor, living in isolated enclaves like Upper Cut Meat
and He Dog, that on food-stamp day, they can obtain transportation to the nearest
supermarket only by paying for it with some of the milk and bread that they intended
to feed their children.

— Belluck, 1997, *New York Times,* September 9, p. A1.

Poor children are affected by an array of powerful risk and protective
influences, many of which are unique to the life circumstance of socioeconomic deprivation. Increasing recognition of such influences has led to
growing exhortations, in the social sciences, for their careful consideration
in theory development, empirical research, interventions, and social policies.
The goal within this volume is to review and synthesize what three decades
of empirical research has taught us about processes that significantly exacerbate or ameliorate the effects of poverty[1] on aspects of children's personal,
emotional, and social development.

The impetus for writing this book stemmed from the recognition of four
factors: (1) increases in national rates of child poverty since the 1970s;
(2) qualitative differences between poverty experiences in recent years as
compared to the first half of the century; (3) recent proliferation of research
on adaptation among disadvantaged children; and (4) evidence of widely
varying profiles of adjustment among poor youth. Since the 1970s, rates of
American children in poverty have been between 20 and 25%: levels substantially higher than the rate of 14% that was achieved during the late 1960s
following the national "war on poverty." Between 1979 and 1994, there was
an addition of almost 2.6 million children to the already high figure of

3.5 million youth under 6 years of age who were growing up in poverty. By 1994, one quarter of the nation's young children were living in conditions of serious socioeconomic disadvantage (National Center for Children in Poverty, 1996).

There have also been changes over time in qualitative experiences of poverty in the United States. Contemporaneously, being poor connotes adversities that were relatively uncommon four to five decades ago (Egeland, Carlson, & Sroufe, 1993; Miringoff, Miringoff, & Opdycke, 1996; National Research Council, 1993; Rogler, 1996). Rates of divorce and of single parent families are higher now than during the 1930s to 1950s. The incidence of teenage motherhood, of substance abuse among families, of family and community violence, and of concentrated poverty in urban neighborhoods, have also increased substantially. Changes such as these imply a substantial difference in the overall experience of life in poverty experienced by children growing up in the 1980s and 1990s, as opposed, for example, to those who experienced the Great Depression (Elder, 1974).

Corresponding with recent increases in child poverty, there has been heightened attention among child development researchers to factors implicated in the psychosocial adjustment of poor children. Whereas in the 1960s and early 1970s, much of the research on disadvantaged youth was focused on their cognitive development, subsequent years have seen increasingly sophisticated studies on facets of social and emotional development (Huston, McLoyd, & Garcia Coll, 1994). This body of research reflects recognition of two interrelated themes, the first of which is that socioeconomic deprivation generally confers risk for maladjustment. Poor children can reflect a threefold or greater risk for major psychiatric disorders as compared to their non-poor counterparts (Costello et al., 1996). On the other hand, there is considerable diversity in adjustment profiles; many children in poverty go on to lead highly productive lives (Garmezy, 1991; Werner & Smith, 1992). Evidence such as this logically leads to questions about the potential antecedents of such varying trajectories—what are the risk and protective processes that substantially mitigate, exacerbate, or mediate, the risks associated with child poverty? It is this question that undergirds the effort undertaken within this volume.

PARAMETERS AND STRUCTURE

The goal in writing this book is to overview a vast body of research evidence to distill salient messages regarding not just the *factors* implicated in poor children's adjustment, but more importantly, the *processes* or *mechanisms* that underlie the documented effects of different forces (Rutter, 1990). The nature of this distinction is perhaps most easily explained with a specific example. Rather than simply concluding that "support from extended kin is helpful for poor children," the emphasis here is on explicating what research has revealed about how and why such an association might inhere. To illustrate, grandparents may provide high levels of emotional support to their grandchildren. Alternatively or additionally, *parents* may benefit from kin support, advantages subsequently reflected in specific parenting behaviors, which in turn are manifested in particular adjustment indices among their children. Understanding such processes underlying risk and protective forces is of obvious value for future efforts across the areas of theory, research, and intervention design.

Perhaps as importantly, if not more so, the aim in reviewing this literature is to draw attention to the innumerable ways in which potentially powerful risk and protective processes do not operate in directions that may be intuitively anticipated, but often can reflect complicated, conditional, and even counterintuitive trends. Reverting to the example cited earlier, for example, researchers have shown that when grandmothers in poverty live in the same household as their unmarried daughters with children, the anticipated benefits of extended kin support can not only be lost, but even reversed, due to various psychological strains on both generations of adults. In recent years, investigators have illuminated numerous such instances wherein salient forces affecting poor children do not operate in unequivocal or straightforward ways. Effects of some forces are conditional on other coexisting circumstances, others are simply contrary to widespread conceptions in mainstream society (and psychology)—yet are eminently understandable when considered in the context of the ecocultural surround.

A central conceptual premise that is interwoven throughout the tapestry of this book, then, is that cultural factors are critical in determining the meanings ascribed to different behaviors (Cohler , Stott, & Musick, 1995; Garcia Coll & Vasquez Garcia, 1995; Weisz, McCarty, Eastman, Chaiyasit, & Suwanlert, 1997). Contextual factors can substantially influence the connotations of psychological constructs, so that the same variable can serve substantial protective functions in one context, yet exacerbate vulnerability in another (Masten, Best, & Garmezy, 1990). The objective here is to identify and discuss those processes which have been found with some consistency, to promote or inhibit salient aspects of social and emotional adjustment among children growing up in poverty.

As used within this volume, the phrase "risk and protective forces" encompasses both mediators and moderators of adverse life circumstances.

Much of this book is focused on elucidating diverse groups of mechanisms that might explain links between poverty and child maladjustment (Adler et al., 1994). Such constructs, commonly known as mediators of risk, are exemplified by high levels of violence in impoverished neighborhoods or psychiatric distress among poor, disenfranchised parents. Also described are various types of moderators, or indices which *interact* with poverty to result in varying child outcomes. Gender is an example of a moderator variable: With exposure to negative socializing influences in their disadvantaged communities, boys are more likely than girls to display problems in adjustment.

The stipulated length of this monograph, and the chosen task of broadly integrating a wealth of empirical findings[2] on risk and protective processes, conjointly preclude in-depth commentary on individual studies cited here. I make no attempts to critique the methodology of specific investigations, in terms of operational definitions and approaches to measurement, sampling, or data analyses. Similarly precluded are analyses of intervention implications for individual areas of risk and protection. Each of these issues, however, is broadly appraised in the last chapter of the book, in which overarching directions for future work are discussed.

This review is focused primarily on empirical evidence on disadvantaged children in the United States during the past three decades.[3] Decisions to remain within these parameters were based in the aforementioned differences in contemporaneous experiences of child poverty in the U.S. as compared to earlier historical eras, as well as substantial differences when compared with other industrialized countries. In 1986 to 1987 when 20% of U.S. children lived in poverty, rates in Sweden were 2% and in Canada, 9% (Danziger & Danziger, 1993). Poor children in the U.S. today also tend to have less of a "safety net" of social programs than their counterparts in other industrialized nations (Lipman & Offord, 1997). Thus, although some research-based conclusions identified in this book may generalize to child poverty experiences in other countries as well, many may be specific to the contextual circumstances and conditions that define child poverty experiences in the contemporary U.S.

Broad-based definitions have been used for the two constructs that anchor this effort; child social-emotional adaptation and poverty. Child outcomes include both behavioral and emotional indices of psychopathology as well as aspects of competence. Factors associated with school achievement (e.g., academic success or dropping out) are considered, although studies focusing strictly on cognitive or language outcomes are not included. A relatively inclusive approach was also used in identifying research involving socioeconomic disadvantage. Most of the studies reviewed here specifically targeted children and families living in poverty, particularly those in inner-city settings. Also included are studies based on more heterogeneous samples, but which yielded information about the specific associations occurring among the more disadvantaged children within the samples. While recognizing that substantial differences in findings can ensue with variations in research designs and approaches to operationalizing major constructs, the effort, again, is to identify themes regarding risk and protective factors that may generalize across investigations with disparate methodologies and samples.

This book is presented in six chapters, including this introduction. Chapters are organized around the three major groups of risk and protective process implicated in resilience among children at risk (Luthar & Zigler, 1991; Masten et al., 1990; Werner & Smith, 1992). These include *child attributes* (Chapter 2), *characteristics of families* (Chapters 3 and 4) and *community-level influences* (Chapter 5). The book concludes with discussions on directions for future scientific efforts involving the adjustment of disadvantaged youth.

SUMMARY

This monograph is focused on factors that might mediate, reduce, or exacerbate the effects of socioeconomic deprivation on children's social-emotional adjustment. This review was undertaken in recognition of recent increases in rates of child poverty, the qualitative differences in experiences of poverty contemporaneously as compared historically, the presence of a burgeoning literature on poor children's adaptation, and evidence that despite the risks linked with poverty, many disadvantaged children show impressive adaptational profiles. The central objective is to integrate findings obtained across three decades of research, to discern meaningful patterns about salient risk and protective processes affecting the social and emotional adjustment of poor children. Recent findings suggest that some aspects of risk and protection operate in straightforward, fairly intuitive ways. However, links involving many others appear to be complicated; the effects of the same variable can differ substantially depending on specific other co-existing contextual factors. In sum, then, the effort within this book is to overview what research has taught us so far, about diverse risk and protective processes affecting poor children—those associated with their own attributes, characteristics of their families, and influences within their wider communities.

NOTES

1. The terms *poverty*, *socioeconomic deprivation*, and *disadvantage* are used interchangeably within this volume.

2. The effort in presenting relevant research is not to conduct an exhaustive literature review, but rather to compile representative findings within each of the major areas of risk and protection.

3. Findings from large-scale, methodologically exemplary studies begun prior to the 1970s are also occasionally cited, both to permit appraisal of historical changes in the ramifications of major risk and protective processes, and to delineate potentially important constructs that have been little explored in recent studies. For similar purposes, some relevant findings from prominent research efforts outside the U.S. are also cited.

2

CHILD ATTRIBUTES

(Deek) preferred the quiet kids: the lean and ragged and hungry ones. It was funny to Ty how those always seemed the darkest too, like himself. They blended into the background, hard to see, but that had little to do with their color. They were more like small and sad-eyed ebony ghosts, haunting the sidewalks or hovering half invisible in doorways or drifting past bars late at night, sighing a soft, almost shy chant of rock, rock, rock, no louder than a breeze stirring trash in the gutter. And no one but the buyers seemed to see them, or hear. Ty also thought it funny how loyal most of them were, like they'd finally found something to believe in after a long, lonely search through a rotting world of hunger and lies, where everything good and everything beautiful was guarded by bars and glass. Sometimes it was hard to tell if the bars locked you in or out.

—Mowry (1993), *Way Past Cool,* pp. 99-100

The psychosocial adjustment profiles of poor youth can show systematic variations depending on various characteristics of the children themselves. Girls and boys can differ substantially, for example, in the degree to which they react to disturbances within their families, as opposed to problems in their neighborhoods and wider communities. Younger children are more susceptible than older ones in several respects. Personal characteristics of children, such as their levels of self-esteem and intelligence, can affect their adjustment across diverse spheres, and the level of adaptational success that children achieve in particular domains can affect their subsequent adjustment across several other domains of development. Empirical evidence regarding each of these indices is reviewed, in turn, in discussions that follow.[1]

GENDER DIFFERENCES IN VULNERABILITY
TO FAMILIAL STRESSORS

Several studies involving youth in poverty have shown that during the early childhood years, boys are more vulnerable than girls to a range of disturbances in family functioning. For example, when children are exposed to high levels of maternal psychopathology during infancy, males more so than females tend to show heightened symptomatology subsequently during childhood (Shaw, Vondra, Hommerding, Keenan, & Dunn, 1994). During the preschool period, boys exposed to high maternal anger and depression display more adjustment difficulties than their female counterparts (Wall & Holden, 1994). Similarly, elementary school boys have been found to be more affected than girls by family economic hardship, as indexed by escalations in levels of externalizing behavior problems (Bolger, Patterson, Thompson, & Kupersmidt, 1995).

Findings of young boys' heightened vulnerability to familial disruptions may often derive from their tendencies to display externalizing symptom patterns. More so than girls, male children tend to express their distress in overt behavior problems such as oppositionality and aggression, rather than internalizing ones such as depression or anxiety (e.g., Bolger et al., 1995; Dodge, Pettit, & Bates, 1994; DuBois, Felner, Meares, & Krier, 1994; Jessor, Van Den Bos, Vanderryn, Costa, & Tubin, 1995; Kazdin, 1995; Luthar, 1995; McLoyd, Jayaratne, Ceballo, & Borquez, 1994). Furthermore, whereas disruptive, oppositional behaviors among children generally elicit negative responses from significant others, these reactions tend to be particularly pronounced when the child concerned is a male. Researchers have found that aggression in boys is particularly likely to elicit negative reactions from peers as well as punitiveness among adults, reactions which in turn can result in additional increases in their maladaptive behavior over time (see Rutter, 1990, for a review).

Among *older* youth in economically deprived families, by contrast, stresses linked with family functioning seem to affect girls more than boys (e.g., Juarez, Viega, & Richards, 1997), perhaps as a result of gender-role socialization. Fathers' rejecting behaviors have been found to affect the psychosocial functioning of adolescent girls but not boys, possibly reflecting, in part, teenage girls' heightened responsibilities in the home (Elder, Nguyen, & Caspi, 1985). Similarly, there is evidence that for disadvantaged adolescent girls more so than boys, stressful experiences involving disturbed interpersonal relationships are linked with heightened coping problems both contemporaneously, as well as subsequently, during adulthood (McGee,

Wolfe, & Wilson, 1997; Werner & Smith, 1992). Findings such as these may derive from the greater propensity of girls, who are typically socialized to be compliant and conciliatory, to be personally distressed by events which involve high interpersonal conflict, hostility, and criticism (Werner & Smith, 1992).

Teenage girls may not only be particularly reactive to interpersonal stressors in the family, but may also feel heightened concern about the well-being of their financially distressed parents. In research on families who experienced the farm crisis of the 1980s, adolescent daughters, more often than sons, expressed concern for their parents and assumed family responsibilities, trends which again were viewed as reflecting gender-linked socialization patterns (Hook, 1990). Boys, on the other hand, reported higher concern about loss of their farm, expressing worries about the future of the family business operation.

The heightened sense of family responsibility among girls may sometimes serve *protective* functions, as suggested by Flanagan (1990) based on findings that parents' employment loss seemed to intensify parent-child conflict more for teenage boys than for girls (see also Conger, Conger, & Elder, 1997). While conceding that such findings may reflect greater reactivity among males (e.g., loss of respect for fathers with unstable employment), Flanagan suggested that girls are more often recruited into family decision-making roles than sons in economically deprived families. This greater autonomy and responsibility may be beneficial for daughters, resulting in relatively positive behavioral adjustment within the home setting.

Although heightened responsibilities in their economically stressed families might be empowering for some girls, there can also be costs. To illustrate, the degree to which single mothers in poverty discuss their personal and financial problems with their children is related to children's levels of emotional distress (McLoyd & Wilson, 1990; 1994). Similarly, when impoverished parents have heightened expectations of their daughters to help in the home, this may often be viewed by girls as low parental support for education and, over time, can lead to reduced levels of engagement at school (Connell, Halpern-Felsher, Clifford, Crichlow, & Usinger, 1995).

For disadvantaged girls (as well as for boys), the potential benefits of premature assumption of adult responsibilities must be carefully weighed against the costs that can accrue across diverse domains of their adjustment. Assuming some adult responsibilities in moderation can certainly help a 14-year-old to feel empowered and strengthened. Yet if these obligations become weighty and inescapable, this can substantially erode the child's psychological well-being, both contemporaneously and in future years, as the assumption of adult responsibilities becomes an increasingly unavoidable reality of life.

Moving away from their families of origin and their roles as sons and daughters, premature assumption of parental roles also affects adjustment trajectories of older girls more so than boys, for the phenomenon of teen parenthood carries more adverse implications for them. Apart from being at elevated risk for medical problems (e.g., due to lack of prenatal care), adolescent mothers more so than fathers assume major responsibilities in caring for their children. Having to juggle child care, education, work, and leisure not only leads to substantial psychological stress, but also increases risks for the teen mother's dropping out of school, and of obtaining employment in subsequent years (Bowman, 1990; Brooks-Gunn & Chase-Lansdale, 1995; Hetherington, 1997).

Noting that relatively few studies have focused specifically on the *psychological* ramifications of teenage pregnancy, Brooks-Gunn and Chase-Lansdale (1995) summarize various challenges in this regard. Aside from heightened vulnerability to depression, negotiating issues of separation can assume critical salience for teen mothers, as strivings for autonomy often coexist with dependence on their own mothers for financial resources, child care, and information about parenthood. Identity development can also be complicated: these youth face the task of constructing a self-definition of motherhood even as they are still constructing self-definitions as independent, sexually mature women. Finally, transition to adolescent motherhood is typically accompanied by several other life changes—in the realms of school, employment, and social status—upheavals which can further exacerbate girls' risks for negative adjustment.

On a more encouraging note, studies have shown that adolescent mothers' long-term educational and employment prospects are not inevitably bleak (Brooks-Gunn & Furstenberg, 1987). The Baltimore study of teenage motherhood, for example, revealed that at a 17 year follow-up, three-fourths of the women were in the work force and only a quarter were on welfare (Brooks-Gunn & Furstenberg, 1987). Among the factors contributing to such positive long-term trajectories, two particularly critical ones were the teenage mother's completion of high school and the degree of spacing between her subsequent children. Teen mothers as well as their children[2] tend to fare relatively well when the mothers delay subsequent childbearing for 2 to 3 years after having had their first-born, ostensibly reflecting the avoidance of additional strains experienced by those young mothers with multiple children, all in the early childhood years (Apfel & Seitz, 1997; Brooks-Gunn & Furstenberg, 1987).

GENDER DIFFERENCES IN VULNERABILITY
TO COMMUNITY-RELATED INFLUENCES

In contrast to age-related gender differences in vulnerability to familial stressors, in the context of reactivity to negative influences in the wider *community*, disadvantaged boys are at greater risk than girls across the developmental span. The greater susceptibility of boys is illustrated within two related bodies of evidence, both involving academic performance. Contrary to trends documented among mainstream youth where boys typically perform at least as well as, if not better than, their female counterparts on standardized achievement tests (Steele, 1997), boys in poverty tend to show poorer outcomes than their female peers, beginning at the elementary school years (Eckenrode, Rowe, Laird, & Braithwaite, 1995). By the high school level, inner-city male students attain lower academic grades as well as poorer teacher ratings of classroom behaviors than females (Luthar, 1995; Ripple & Luthar, 1998). In research involving African American[3] teens from multiple urban locations in the U.S., boys consistently fared more poorly than girls on a composite construct of low attendance, low achievement scores and grades, suspension, and retention at school (Connell, Spencer, & Aber, 1994).

Coexisting with this evidence of poorer academic prognosis among boys in poverty are data indicating that community influences can be substantially implicated. To illustrate, among elementary school children in Baltimore, neighborhood resources, such as the presence of mostly low-income versus more affluent neighbors, were more strongly linked with the achievement test scores of boys than those of girls (Entwisle, Alexander & Olson, 1994). Results of the Woodlawn longitudinal study in Chicago (Ensminger, Lamkin, & Jacobson, 1996) indicated that male African American teens who lived in middle-class neighborhoods were more likely than others to graduate from high school, even after considering various familial and personal characteristics. These neighborhood effects were not found for girls. Similarly, direct associations have been reported between aspects of the ecological setting and educational and psychosocial outcomes among African American boys (but not girls), even after considering effects linked with family support and diverse personal attributes (Connell et al., 1995).

Findings of such gender differences have typically been interpreted in terms of the greater exposure of boys to community-level forces. As compared to girls, boys are more likely to participate in neighborhood activities and can thus benefit more from high levels of resources in their communities, as in affluent neighborhoods (Entwisle et al., 1994). Concomitantly, girls are more likely to be restricted to the home in dangerous inner-city neighborhoods, and thus remain more shielded than their male counterparts from negative community influences (Ensminger et al., 1996), including those reflecting flagrant repudiation of academic effort and achievement. As Wilson (1987) has argued, inner-city youngsters who remain isolated from mainstream values on education and work (due to middle-class migration from poor urban areas), typically become increasingly disinterested in schooling and employment. This, in turn, results in their increasing involvement in deviant and criminal activities. In a similar vein are suggestions that inner-city boys who perform poorly at school begin to remove themselves from the socializing influences of teachers and schools, and become increasingly vulnerable to antisocial forces within their communities (Lynam, Moffitt, & Stouthamer-Loeber, 1993). Negative community-based influences such as these are often particularly harmful for ethnic minority boys (as will be shown in Chapter 3); yet there is little doubt that for inner-city boys in general, the "world of the streets" has potent influences across the years of childhood and adolescence, spanning multiple aspects of their educational as well as personal-social adjustment.

AGE DIFFERENCES

In preceding discussions, effects involving age have generally been discussed in terms of conditional associations—that is, those depending on the child's gender—but what of "main effects" for age? Are younger children, for instance, typically hurt more so than older ones by the life circumstance of family poverty?[4]

Without question, younger children, being relatively defenseless, are more vulnerable than older youth in many respects. Experiences of chronic poverty during early childhood inhibit subsequent educational outcomes as well as employment during adulthood, to a greater degree than exposure to poverty in the later childhood years (Duncan & Brooks-Gunn, 1997a). In a similar vein, younger children in poverty tend to show greater vulnerability than older ones to depressive symptoms. Although the incidence of depression goes up dramatically between the ages of 11 and 15 years in the general population (McGee, Feehan, Williams, & Anderson, 1992), studies with poor children have indicated greater distress among pre-pubertal youth versus early adolescents (Fitzpatrick, 1993), and among younger teens as compared to older ones (McLoyd & Wilson, 1990; Ripple & Luthar, 1998).

Trends such as these may reflect less mature coping strategies and fewer psychological resources among younger children, as well as fewer social outlets (which in turn would potentially increase exposure to negative home experiences) (McLoyd & Wilson, 1990). It is also possible that once children start to attend school, they are often exposed to potentially important compensatory influences that can mitigate against the effects of family poverty. In other words, support from individuals outside the family, such as parents, teachers, or friends, may become increasingly salient as children progress along the developmental continuum, possibly overriding the salience of family socioeconomic disadvantage in itself (Duncan and Brooks-Gunn, 1997b).

The expansion of poor children's social worlds to extra-familial realms can also, however, have a range of *negative* consequences. Increasing freedom to explore the wider community can bring greater exposure to negative lifestyles and role models in inner-city settings, and can result, as well, in ever-sharpening awareness of the many ways in which their life circumstances differ from those of more privileged youth. Consequences of these "new risks" may often lie less in self-reported depressive symptoms among older children, and more in their increasing involvement, over time, in counter-conventional behaviors. Many disadvantaged children show significant increases in behavior problems at school across the preschool and mid-elementary years (Dodge, Pettit, & Bates, 1994). Similarly, junior high and high school students show escalating maladjustment with age in various domains including detachment from academics and increases in problems of substance use, delinquency, and sexuality (Jessor et al., 1995; Lempers, Clark-Lempers, & Simons, 1989; Ripple & Luthar, 1998).

Findings such as these underscore the need for far greater attentiveness than is typically accorded, to the mental health difficulties of older children in disadvantaged settings. To be sure, developmental increases in rebellious, anti-establishment behaviors are not necessarily unique to poverty; they may partly reflect changes that generally occur across childhood including increasing predilections toward antisocial behaviors during adolescence (e.g., Moffitt, 1993a). This caveat notwithstanding, existing evidence sharply calls into question widespread tendencies, among social scientists as well as others (see McLoyd, 1997), to consider only children in the early childhood years as those that are seriously affected by family socioeconomic disadvantage. "Deviant" behavior patterns among older youth in poverty do not inevitably represent wanton and willful acts of destructiveness, but can equally be manifestations of high personal distress. As suggested at the outset of this chapter, many such behaviors reflect the consequences, rather than the causes, of years of unrelenting deprivation and alienation from the incentives and rewards of mainstream society.

PERSONAL CHARACTERISTICS

Intelligence

High intelligence is often salient in distinguishing relatively well-adapted at-risk youth from those who achieve less positive outcomes (Fergusson & Lynskey, 1996; Luthar & Zigler, 1991; Masten et al., 1990; Smith & Prior, 1995; Werner & Smith, 1992). In terms of underlying mechanisms, a high IQ may involve strengths in problem-solving and coping, wherein bright children may be better able to evaluate consequences of their behaviors, to delay gratification, and to contain impulses. Additionally, IQ may be protective because of the benefits associated with repeated academic successes, given the strong emphasis in schooling in contemporary society.

Although a high IQ generally presages positive outcomes, overall advantages can be attenuated in the presence of adverse circumstances such as high levels of life stress. In research involving inner-city adolescents, bright teens generally fared better than their less intelligent classmates across various indices of school-based competence. However, in the presence of various negative forces (such as high life stress or high levels of emotional distress), they lost much of their advantage so that their performance at school more closely approximated that of their less intelligent peers (see Luthar, 1997, for an overview of these studies).

Collectively, findings such as these may indicate the greater sensitivity of intelligent children to both environmental and intrapsychic forces. Bright inner-city children, like intelligent children in general, may be more keenly attuned than others to the vicissitudes of their life experiences, reacting more adversely to negative influences and benefitting more from positive ones. Equally, however, these findings may reflect a relatively tenuous commitment to traditional mainstream schooling—generally viewed as irrelevant for future success by many bright inner-city youth (see also Chapter 3)—and their consciousness, concomitantly, of the substantial immediate rewards to be gained by investment of talents in entrepreneurial efforts (including illegal ones) in their neighborhoods and communities.

Temperament

Infants who are viewed as good-natured, active, and cuddly, tend to be among those children who later reflect resilience in psychosocial outcomes, as opposed to relative maladjustment, in the face of multiple socio-demographic disadvantages (Werner & Smith, 1992; Wyman, Cowen, Work, & Parker, 1991). Among school-age children in poverty, similarly, teacher ratings of positive temperament have been found to be among the best discriminators of resilient functioning across multiple behavioral domains (Smith & Prior, 1995).

Conversely, difficult temperament can increase the risks associated with life in poverty, by exacerbating, for example, negative reactions from caregivers (Farber & Egeland, 1987). Research findings on bidirectional links between maltreatment and children's adjustment indicate that whereas maltreated infants tend to display greater disturbance than adequately reared low socio-economic status (SES) children, these behavioral disturbances are unlikely to be responsible for the *initiation* of maltreatment. At the same time, deviant infant behaviors may often contribute to the *maintenance* of maltreatment after it has been initiated by the mother (Crittenden, 1985). Among school-age children in economically stressed families, similarly, those with difficult temperaments are more likely than others to receive harsh, punitive, or detached patterns of discipline from their parents (Elder, Liker, & Cross, 1984).

Although difficult temperaments are more often linked with negative long-term outcomes than are easy ones, this is not invariably the case. Arguing this point, Rutter (1989a) cited a provocative study by de Vries (1984) on Masai infants which showed that in the life-threatening circumstances of severe drought, difficult babies were more likely to survive than were easy ones. Explanations raised included the possibility that the more demanding babies were more likely to receive care necessary for survival, and/or that difficult infants may not have presented as much of a problem in Masai culture where assertiveness is a valued trait, and multiple caregivers are available given an extended family structure (de Vries, 1984; Rutter, 1989a).

Locus of control

Protective effects for disadvantaged youth have been found for *internal locus of control,* or the belief that events in one's life are largely shaped by one's own efforts and actions, rather than external forces such as luck or destiny (Werner & Smith, 1992). Among inner-city high school students, those with an internal locus of control, but not their more externally oriented counterparts, have been found to display relative stability in behavioral and emotional functioning regardless of high versus low levels of recent negative life events (Luthar, 1991; Weist, Freedman, Paskewitz, Proescher, & Flaherty, 1995). These findings may partly reflect variations in coping styles. Youngsters who believe that events in their lives are largely controllable may actively attempt to overcome everyday adversities, employing coping strategies which tend to promote positive outcomes across diverse areas of adaptation (Luthar, 1991; Wyman, Cowen, Work, & Kerley, 1993).

A postulate insufficiently explored in existing empirical research is that an internal locus of control may not be unequivocally beneficial for disadvantaged youth. Tendencies to assume responsibility for their failures may often be extreme and intrapunitive among children growing up in poverty, who encounter several social constraints linked with their lower-class status (and often, coexisting minority status as well). In other words, whereas external locus of control may often be a valid sign of fatalism and learned helplessness, it can equally signal some inner-city individuals' recognition of the systematic and real obstacles against their achievement in society. The benefits of disadvantaged children's willingness to assume personal responsibility for their failures must therefore be carefully weighed against the merits of their flexibly and realistically acknowledging externally-imposed obstacles which they, more than their more affluent counterparts, must contend with on an ongoing basis.

Other Attributes

Children who have *high self-esteem* and *self-efficacy* are more likely than others to show resilient adaptational outcomes (see Spencer, Cole, DuPree, Glymph, & Pierre, 1993; Werner & Smith, 1992). Among African American youth, high levels of self-worth have been found to be related to positive educational outcomes such as regularity of school attendance and good grades (Connell et al., 1994). Similarly, among multiply disadvantaged school-age children, protective effects have been demonstrated for high self-esteem, as well as *ego resiliency* and *ego control*, in relation to adaptive functioning across diverse domains including school performance, self-reported mental health, and relationships with adults and peers (Cicchetti, Rogosch, Lynch, & Holt, 1993). Various mechanisms might underlie such findings involving self-system constructs. In the face of adversities, children with high self-esteem may be less prone than others to depressive symptomatology, and might be more likely to retain convictions in their own capacities to master challenges. Similarly, children with high levels of ego control and ego resiliency are more likely than others to be able to flexibly modulate their feelings, impulses, and desires in response to demands and obstacles encountered in daily life situations (Block & Block, 1980; Cicchetti et al., 1993).

In the realm of interpersonal skills, protective influences have been found for *social problem-solving abilities* as well as *social expressiveness* among poor children (Cowen, Work, & Wyman, 1997; Luthar, 1991; Werner & Smith, 1992). In research conducted with delinquent, runaway, and disadvantaged adolescent males, the developmental sophistication of boys' interpersonal negotiation strategies was significantly linked with various problem behaviors including drug use and delinquency (Leadbeater, Hellner, Allen, & Aber, 1989). Findings such as these attest to the importance of children's capacities to consider both their own needs and others' in negotiating interpersonal conflicts. At-risk youngsters who are facile at collaboratively working through everyday conflict situations are less likely than others to come to display recurrent unruly, disruptive patterns of behavior.

In a related vein, *negative* aspects of social-cognitive functioning can heighten risks among disadvantaged youth. Among low-income, African American elementary school boys, attributional biases have been found to underlie children's own levels of aggressiveness as well as their responsiveness to aggression in peers (Graham & Hoehn, 1995; Graham & Hudley, 1994). For example, the aggressive children tended to be particularly quick to assume intentionality underlying peers' aggression, even when such assumptions were unwarranted. Misattributions such as these often result from ready access to relatively biased causal constructs in the child's memory. When children's own life histories are replete with instances of receiving and assigning blame, they can become, over time, quick to infer intentional aggression in others (Graham & Hudley, 1994).

Research on Child Attributes: Inferences and Implications

Before closing discussions on children's personal attributes as risk or protective factors, a word of caution is necessary regarding a potentially damaging misinterpretation that can arise, that is, if poor children's own characteristics significantly affect their overall adaptation, it follows that those who do poorly are themselves responsible for their negative life trajectories. Some scholars have argued, in fact, it can be dangerous for researchers even to focus on child attributes in resilience, for this can promote tendencies to "blame the victim" and suggestions that if only at-risk children had particular traits or skills, they could do well in life (Tarter & Vanyukov, in press; Tolan, 1996). Two points should be noted with regard to this undoubtedly important concern.

First, evidence that a child characteristic is involved in problem behaviors by no means implies placing the onus or blame with the child. Aside from biological, neuropsychological, and genetic factors (e.g., Moffitt, 1993b; Quay, 1993; Plomin, 1995), children's social-cognitive and interpersonal predilections are borne from years of experiences in their social milieus. To consider attributional biases in aggression, for example, a child's readiness to assume intentionality for others' aggression often represents a genuine strategy for coping with the vicissitudes of daily life in poverty. With frequent use, strategies such as these become part of how youngsters generally interpret their social worlds, extending to situations when they are unnecessary or inappropriate (Graham & Hudley, 1994).

Second, from the perspective of both theory and interventions, there is much to be gained from research that is aimed at understanding the specific aspects of children's personal functioning that tend to exacerbate their adjustment problems. Returning again to evidence on attributional biases, Graham's findings illuminate some precise facets of children's habitual ways of interpreting environmental cues that significantly contribute to escalations in aggression; thereby illuminating a delimited, and what is more important, a relatively "modifiable" set, of underlying processes.

In sum, scientific attention to child attributes in resilience and vulnerability does not connote predilections to assign responsibility or blame. It helps to identify the specific aspects of children's habitual ways of responding to life events that might underlie broad behavioral profiles of adaptation. Furthermore, this is an exercise of value not only for researchers seeking to understand underlying processes, but also for clinicians and teachers interested in identifying useful target points for preventive interventions.

TRAJECTORIES OF ADJUSTMENT

A child's adjustment profile at a particular stage of development can carry substantial prognostic significance for his or her adaptation in subsequent years. Structural-organizational perspectives of child development (Cicchetti & Toth, 1995; Sroufe & Rutter, 1984) maintain that there is general coherence in the unfolding of competence over time, such that achieving success at particular stage-salient developmental tasks can give children a foundation of success or failure from which they approach future developmental challenges. The notion of heterotypic continuity (Kagan, 1971), similarly, carries the implication that particular forms of child maladjustment often eventuate in adjustment difficulties across several other conceptually related domains. Relevant findings from research on poor children are reviewed in discussions that follow.

Continuities in Competence

Consistent with structural-organizational theories, studies with disadvantaged youth have established that a history of competent development has substantial protective effects for long-term adjustment. Data from the Minnesota Mother-Child Research Project have shown that for boys of mothers experiencing high life stress, competence during infancy and early childhood was significantly linked with positive adaptation in elementary school (Egeland & Kreutzer, 1991). Positive adjustment prior to toddlerhood retained protective effects for subsequent school-based competence, even among those children who had displayed intermittent adjustment setbacks during the intervening period (i.e., at 3 or 4 years of age) (Sroufe, Egeland, & Kreutzer, 1990).

Similar protective influences are evident in research on early educational adaptation (Reynolds, 1998). In longitudinal research involving African American children, cognitive competence and academic motivation levels during kindergarten were predictive of achievement scores during elementary school, which in turn, were linked with how long children remained at school (Luster & McAdoo, 1996). In a similar vein, educational competence during junior high and on entry into high school is significantly related to the likelihood of completing high school (Connell et al., 1995; Finn & Rock, 1997; Ripple & Luthar, 1998). Thus, inner-city youth who are engaged with academic effort on their entry into high school (as indexed, for example, by regular attendance, infrequent suspensions, and good grades) are far less likely than others to drop out before completing their high school education.

The benefits of history of competence can extend well into the adult years. In the Harvard Study of Adult Development, in which over 400 disadvantaged males were followed since early adolescence (Felsman & Vaillant, 1987), a composite construct of boyhood competence was found to be the strongest overall predictor of subsequent adult adjustment during middle age. Even protective influences encountered during early adulthood can alter subsequent adjustment trajectories. Among women who were institutionalized as children, Rutter (1990) found that marriage to a nondeviant, supportive spouse was a critical factor in discriminating between those who showed relatively positive versus negative outcomes subsequently in adulthood. For the long term adjustment of individuals in poverty, these findings collectively underscore the value of facilitating movement toward positive trajectories not only during the incontrovertibly critical period of early childhood, but also at subsequent points in development during the grade school years, adolescence, and adulthood.

Cross-Domain Continuities and Discontinuities

Studies of cross-domain associations among poor youth have frequently been focused on one of two broad themes: links involving children's substance use and other social-emotional adjustment indices, and associations among different facets of their behavioral and academic adjustment at school. In general, results have indicated that a particular "deviant" behavior will presage significant problems across other adjustment domains largely to the degree that the earlier-appearing behavior represents high deviance in the immediate subcultural context, and not just vis-à-vis definitions of maladjustment by mainstream norms.

Consider substance abuse. Several studies have shown that among disadvantaged youth, baseline levels of drug and alcohol use are significantly linked with subsequent problems across the realms of academic, behavioral, and emotional adjustment, as reported by various informants (Allen, Leadbeater, & Aber, 1994; Brunswick, Lewis, & Messeri, 1991; Luthar & Cushing 1997). Interestingly, there is little evidence of associations in the opposite direction, e.g., from early academic difficulties or self-reported depression, to subsequent problems of drug use. These data suggest two possibilities. First, substance use among many inner-city youth may not derive predominantly from personal maladjustment, but might often reflect factors external to the child such as high accessibility of drugs in the neighborhood and frequent substance use among significant others in the environment (National Research Council, 1993). Second, as noted earlier, the contextual deviance of a particular behavior partially determines the likelihood of whether it will eventuate in other forms of serious maladjustment. Thus, while students who frequently use illegal drugs may well develop other problems such as academic failure, it is less likely that all inner-city teens who are not invested in academics will go on to abuse illegal drugs.

Similarly, problems in one aspect of poor-children's school-based functioning do not inevitably spell difficulties across other areas. Several studies on mainstream youth have indicated that children who are unpopular with peers in the classroom develop problems in many other areas at school, including academic difficulties (see Luthar, 1995, for a review). In the inner-city setting, by contrast, adolescents with *positive* status in the peer group can be among the most susceptible to later academic problems. Luthar (1995) found that inner-city teenagers viewed as highly sociable by their classmates early in the year showed significant decreases in school grades in subsequent months; conversely, those initially viewed as responsible and behaviorally acquiescent tended to earn poor peer ratings on sociability by the end of the school year.

Reviewing these and related findings, Luthar (1997) suggested that among disadvantaged urban youth, coherence in the unfolding of competence over time is likely to be displayed within, though not necessarily across, distinct groups of behaviors: those reflecting allegiance to the values of mainstream society versus those endorsed by the immediate subculture. On the one hand, youngsters in inner-city settings are confronted with mainstream society's emphasis on academic success and behavioral conformity. On the other hand are sentiments among peers in the inner-city subculture, who—given widespread disillusionment that academic effort will actually promote long-term success—often repudiate conformity to mainstream conventions. Given these antagonistic value systems, children whose early behaviors reflect compliance with mainstream society's rules and standards (e.g., those highly motivated to succeed academically) are likely to continue on this path. Conversely, without external intervention, youngsters who reject conventional means of achieving success (e.g., the "Cool Cats" and "Gowsters/ Antagonists" that Ogbu (1988) has written about) are likely to identify increasingly, over time, with the values and rewards that are preeminent within their disenfranchised urban communities.

In sum, poor children who show positive adjustment patterns early in development generally fare better than others in later years as well. However, this by no means implies that youngsters who experience difficulties as adolescents are doomed to poor long-term outcomes, for research has shown that with appropriate support, even young adults in poverty can move from relatively negative trajectories toward more positive ones. Finally, the likelihood of observing heterotypic continuity of problem behaviors among poor youth is partially determined by the level of contextual deviance that is reflected by the ontogenetically earlier-occurring "maladaptive" behavior.

SUMMARY

1. Early in development, young boys in poverty often reflect greater maladjustment than girls in relation to disturbances in family functioning. After adolescence, however, girls are more vulnerable. For many teenage girls, strains linked with heightened feelings of responsibility for family members—economically stressed parents as well as, often, their own children— can strain aspects of their own psychological development.

In terms of risks linked with negative community influences, conversely, disadvantaged boys are more vulnerable than girls across the developmental spectrum. Their greater susceptibility is frequently reflected in boys' relative disengagement from academic schooling, which in turn can lead to several other problems including increasing involvement in delinquency and crime.

2. Given their limited defenses and coping resources, young children are particularly vulnerable to the exigencies of chronic family poverty; they frequently show higher levels of emotional distress than their older counterparts. Among adolescents, by contrast, the toll of life in poverty may be most starkly manifested in their increasing alienation, over time, from the norms, sanctions, and rewards of mainstream society.

3. Like bright children in general, intelligent children in poverty tend to fare better at school than their less intelligent peers. Their commitment to excelling at school can, however, be more tenuous. Particularly as they approach adolescence, many gifted youth in poverty may be tempted to bring their talents to pursuits far removed from the confines of school, resulting in an increase in their personal vulnerability as well as a tremendous forfeiture of human potential for society.

Easygoing temperaments are generally protective for long-term adaptation; yet poor children who are demanding and assertive can be more successful at getting some of their needs met than their relatively acquiescent counterparts. Other personal attributes that often serve protective functions include internal locus of control, sophisticated interpersonal skills and negotiation strategies, and high self-esteem—aspects of poor children's self-development which in turn are often largely shaped by the timbre of both prior and current life experiences.

4. In general, attaining positive adjustment at any point on the developmental continuum, not only during early childhood, augurs well for later adjustment across related domains. However, a particular form of "maladjustment" heralds serious psychopathology across other domains partly to the degree that it reflects deviance from salient values and norms in the immediate subculture. Similarly, divergences in major microcosmic (e.g., inner-city) and macrocosmic (mainstream) socializing influences can constrain the degree to which "competence" achieved within one domain of adjustment will promote successful adaptation in other important areas.

NOTES

1. Risk and protective processes linked with child ethnicity are not considered here but are described in the following chapter, in the interest of maintaining continuity in discussions

concerning ethnicity vis-à-vis adaptation among parents in poverty as well as among their children.

2. Disturbances in teenage mothers' parenting behaviors and in their children's outcomes are discussed in the next chapter on effects associated with families' sociodemographic characteristics.

3. The terms *African American* and *black* are used interchangeably throughout this book.

4. Discussions here focus on specific age-related vulnerabilities to poverty. It should also be noted, however, that the ill-effects of family poverty are substantially stronger the longer children are exposed to it. Persistent family poverty, which endures for a period of several years, has significantly worse implications for both psychological and academic outcomes among children than does deprivation that is transient or intermittent (see Bolger et al., 1995; Brooks-Gunn, 1995; Duncan, Brooks-Gunn, & Klebanov, 1994; Egeland et al., 1993).

3

POVERTY AND THE FAMILY

Demographic and Structural Features

> I thought about stories I'd been told, about women whose men left them or stayed to laugh out the sides of their mouths when other men mentioned other women's names. Behind my aunt Dot was a legion of female cousins and great-aunts, unknown and nameless—snuff-sucking, empty-faced creatures changing spindles at the textile plant, chewing gum while frying potatoes at the truck stop, exhausted, angry, and never loved enough.
>
> The women I loved most in the world horrified me. I did not want to grow up to be them. I made myself proud of their pride, their determination, their stubbornness, but every night I prayed a man's prayer: Lord, save me from them. Do not let me become them.
>
> —Allison, 1995, *Two or Three Things I Know for Sure,* pp. 37-38.

Various characteristics of their parents and families can affect personal and social outcomes among youngsters growing up in poverty. Patterns of adaptation may show systematic variations depending on the demographic and structural composition of children's families, as well as multiple facets of parents' mental health and parenting behaviors.

Given the breadth of relevant research evidence on familial factors affecting poor children, these constructs are discussed in this chapter as well as in the one that follows. The focus in this chapter is on sociodemographic characteristics, including maternal age, family structure, and several facets of ethnic group membership, whereas the next chapter is devoted to psychological characteristics of disadvantaged parents. Two themes undergird discussions that follow here: (1) effects of particular indices on the functioning of parents, and (2) direct associations of these indices with aspects of children's functioning.

TEENAGE MOTHERS

Families led by young, never-married mothers are overrepresented among families living in poverty,[1] and teen mothers can be at heightened risk not only in terms of their own adjustment trajectories (as indicated in the previous chapter), but also in terms of their parenting attitudes and behaviors. As compared to adult mothers, adolescent parents tend to be more insensitive and impatient with their infants, have less realistic expectations, and provide less responsive, stimulating affective environments for their children (see Brooks-Gunn & Chase-Lansdale, 1995). Similarly, with their older children, younger mothers are more likely to use parent-oriented disciplinary strategies such as physical punishment or removal of privileges, as opposed to child-oriented strategies such as reasoning (Kelley, Power, & Wimbush, 1992; McLanahan & Sandefur, 1994).

Some have suggested, however, that failure to consider other facets of mothers' background may often result in overestimations of the degree to which young age in itself represents heightened risk for negative maternal outcomes (see Brooks-Gunn & Chase-Lansdale, 1995; Geronimus & Korenman, 1992). In many studies, teenage mothers have been compared with women differing from them not only in age but also on other indices such as marital status, employment, education, or verbal ability. After indices such as these have been considered, maternal age tends to show only weak associations with mothers' personal adjustment as well as their parenting behaviors (Chase-Lansdale, Brooks-Gunn, & Zamsky, 1994; Reis, Barbera-Stein, & Bennett, 1986; Wasserman, Rauh, Brunelli, Garcia-Castro, & Necos, 1990).

Contextual factors can also be critical in determining the ramifications of teen pregnancy. To illustrate, ethnographic evidence indicates that for many girls in inner-city areas, adolescent motherhood can represent a cherished symbol of adult status (Burton, Allison, & Obeidallah, 1995). Similarly, Garcia Coll and colleagues (1996) have argued that among traditional, low-SES families in Puerto Rico, teen mothers are typically married, have planned pregnancies, and have access to a support system of women who themselves had been adolescent parents. Consonant with these assertions, research by this group has shown that the implications of teen parenthood—for both mothers and their infants—are less negative among low-SES Puerto Rican mothers than for their U.S. counterparts (see Garcia Coll & Vasquez Garcia, 1995 for a review).

In general, *children* of teen mothers show negative outcomes more consistently than do their mothers, even after considering other social factors (Hetherington, 1997). As compared to children of older parents, offspring of adolescent mothers are more prone to developing a range of problems by their middle school years such as hyperactivity, school misbehavior, delinquency, and substance abuse (Brooks-Gunn & Furstenberg, 1987; Osborn, 1990). In their longitudinal research, Apfel and Seitz (1997) found that although some children of teenage African American mothers performed surprisingly well academically by the age of 12, even these apparently "resilient" youngsters manifested substantial social-emotional problems such as high aggressiveness and underlying hostility and anger. Notwithstanding the relatively positive outcomes eventually achieved by some adolescent mothers (Chapter 2), therefore, the high costs of teenage parenthood are clearly evident in the range of problems documented among their children.

FAMILY STRUCTURE

Single-Parent Households

Moving from the effects of teenage parenthood in particular to those of single parenthood in general, several studies have shown that poor children of single mothers are vulnerable across many spheres of psychological adjustment (see McLanahan, 1997; National Research Council, 1993; Offord, Boyle, & Racine, 1991). Even after considering income levels, these youngsters are at elevated risk for problems in emotional, behavioral, and academic adjustment, with risks particularly high among children of never-married or divorced mothers (as opposed to widowed parents).

Some studies of African American youth, however, have suggested that single parent family status does not inevitably confer high risk for child maladjustment. In an investigation involving three independent samples of urban, African American teens, for example, female-headed family status was unrelated to several indices of adolescent adaptation, such as facets of self-system processes (e.g., perceived self-worth), as well as educational outcomes including achievement scores, attendance levels, and frequency of suspensions (Connell et al., 1994).

More strikingly, Zimmerman, Salem, and Maton (1995) found that inner-city, African American adolescent males living in single mother homes reported *greater* support from their parents than other boys. The authors suggested that single mothers may work harder to provide their sons with support to compensate for the absence of fathers. Furthermore, many sons of single mothers may continue to receive support from their fathers, even when fathers live in different households: As many as two-thirds of the "father-absent" boys in the Zimmerman study reported that their fathers served as their primary male role models. Data such as these question widespread stereotypes about fathers in poor families, suggesting that even when es-tranged from their families of procreation, many can have substantial con-cerns about their role as parents and can significantly affect the well-being of their children (see also Luster and McAdoo, 1994; Luthar, Cushing, & McMahon, 1997).

Coresidence of Extended Kin

Early studies (e.g., Kellam, Ensminger, & Turner, 1977) showed that grandmothers' coresidence with single mothers—also common among dis-advantaged families—served protective functions, ostensibly because shar-ing child-rearing responsibilities with another adult can reduce mothers' feelings of isolation and allow for better quality of child care. Among African American lower- to lower-middle class families, grandmothers who lived with their single-parent daughters were found to be significantly more active in both supporting and controlling their grandchildren than grandmothers who lived in the community (Wilson, 1984).

More recent evidence suggests, however, that kin coresidence in itself can not only have negligible beneficial effects (Burchinal, Follmer, & Bryant, 1996), but may sometimes even have *negative* repercussions. In the Baltimore Multigenerational Study, Chase-Lansdale and colleagues (1994) found that mother-grandmother coresidence seemed to adversely affect the quality of parenting by mothers in poverty, particularly when they were young adults as opposed to teenagers. Explanations rested on the possibility that conflict may be heightened due to sharing of child-rearing responsibilities, and that there may be a diffusion of responsibilities when the adults each assume that the onus of caring for the child rests with the other (Chase-Lansdale et al., 1994). Findings such as these may also reflect escalations in conflict between caretakers that result simply from living in close proximity within confined physical space (Nitz, Ketterlinus, & Brandt, 1995).

Chase-Lansdale and colleagues (1994) also found overall negative effects of co-residence on *grandmothers'* parenting, which they explained in terms of the drain placed on grandmothers' resources. African American grandmothers in multi-generational families are often forced to balance several demands including those linked with adult midlife roles, new responsibilities of caring for the next generation, and frequently, economic hardship with the attendant stressors (Apfel & Seitz, 1997; Burton, 1990). Aside from potential disturbances in mother-grandmother relationships and in the child-rearing behaviors of both generations, therefore, demands imposed on grandparents' resources represent another dimension in which kin-coresidence can place strains on the adaptation of families in poverty.

ETHNICITY

Noting that in general, there is a disproportionate representation of minority individuals among the lower socioeconomic strata of American society, disadvantage is frequently discussed in the context of the dual criteria of non-Caucasian ethnicity and economic subordination (McLoyd, 1990; Ogbu, 1988). Some have argued against treating poverty and ethnicity as synonymous, however, and have called for the examination of developmental processes that might be unique to particular ethnic groups (e.g., MacPhee, Kreutzer, & Fritz, 1994). The remainder of this chapter is focused on processes that might generalize across ethnically diverse families in poverty, as opposed to those that seem to be largely distinctive to specific subgroups.

Variations in Parents' Socialization Goals

Across different ethnic groups, parents can vary greatly in their *socialization goals,* or what they value about their children's emotions and behaviors. Reviewing such differences, Garcia Coll, Meyer, and Brillon (1995) note that among African American families, child-rearing priorities often include fostering children's sense of personal identity with their cultural heritage and belongingness to the broader kinship network. Among Asian Americans, major child-rearing goals include self-control, morality and character development, as well as formal education. Enduring traditional values among Hispanic Americans include a deep sense of family loyalty, an emphasis on interpersonal relatedness, and on inner dignity and respect of the individual as opposed to social and economic standing.

In an empirical effort to disentangle the relative contributions of Hispanic culture versus SES to parents' socialization beliefs, Harwood and colleagues found that although each made independent contributions, cultural effects were stronger. Despite some within-group variability linked with high versus low socioeconomic levels, Anglo mothers generally placed more value on socializing children toward developing self-confidence, independence, and autonomy, whereas the socialization goals of Puerto Rican mothers more strongly emphasized respectful, obedient, and polite behaviors (Harwood, Schoelmerich, Ventura-Cook, Schulze, & Wilson, 1996).

In considering ethnicity and parenting, an intriguing question is whether the *implications* of particular parenting behaviors might differ across different ethnic groups: might the constituents of effective versus detrimental parenting vary depending on ethnicity? Relevant to this query are findings that although disadvantaged African American parents may often be more critical and controlling than Caucasians, the strategies they use seem to be conducive to children's mental health (Baldwin et al., 1993). "African American families are tougher on their kids, but this child-rearing strategy works; that is, it produces children with higher mental health" (p. 758).

In a related vein, recent evidence has shown that in terms of links with children's problem behaviors, optimal levels of control exerted by African American parents vary according to negative influences in the broader community. When adolescents report relatively high problem behaviors in their peer groups, for example, optimal levels of parental control tend to be higher, than when children's peer problem behaviors are low (Mason, Cauce, Gonzales, & Hiraga, 1996). These and similar data (Baumrind, 1972; Mason, Cauce, Gonzales, Hiraga, & Grove, 1994), have led to suggestions that the notion of authoritative parenting is not an appropriate descriptor for "good parenting" among African-American families (Mason et al., 1996). For many African American families in inner-city settings whose children are exposed to high levels of deviance in the wider community, high parental control does not represent "overcontrolling" behavior, but instead is an adaptive parenting strategy, bringing order, predictability, and safety to the everyday lives of their children.

Caveats to such inferences are seen in a paper by Rowe, Vazsonyi, and Flannery (1994), provocatively entitled, "No more than skin deep: Ethnic and racial similarity in developmental processes." These authors analyzed six diverse data sources and showed that although *average levels* of family variables and child outcomes might differ across ethnic groups, the pattern of *associations* among them does not. Stated differently, their analyses suggested that developmental processes were nearly identical across different ethnic groups; group average differences in particular outcomes may often result simply from different levels of (the same set of) antecedent variables. Based on their findings, Rowe and colleagues (1994) cautioned against hasty inferences about ethnic differences in developmental processes, and underscored the need for such conclusions to be rooted in clearly stated prior research hypotheses, replications across independent samples, and appropriate statistical analyses (e.g., with differences inferred from interaction terms rather than on the presence of effects in one group but not the other).

Effects of Poverty on Minority Families

Minority families are over-represented among poverty groups and also experience particularly persistent and extreme forms of poverty (McLoyd, 1990). Forty-two percent of all African American children and 40% of Hispanic children live below the national poverty level,[2] as compared with 16% of White children (Bauger & Lamison-White, 1996). Persistent poverty, remaining below the poverty line for at least 10 of 15 years, afflicts nearly one-quarter of African American youth as opposed to almost no Caucasian children (Duncan, 1994). If poor, minority group children are more likely than Caucasians to live in neighborhoods where institutional supports for families and children are meager (Duncan et al., 1994).

Given their exposure to relatively extreme forms of poverty, along with additional stressors related to discrimination and thwarted mobility aspirations, low-SES minority parents may be expected to show greater psychiatric distress than their Caucasian counterparts. In a direct test of the overlap between ethnicity and poverty status, Kessler and Neighbors (1986) found an interactive effect which suggested, in fact, that the ill-effects of poverty on mental health status were more pronounced among African Americans than Caucasians.

Although reactions to their additional adversities might also be expected in minority individuals' parenting behaviors, evidence in this regard is mixed. Noting historically negative stereotypes about minority families, Kelley, Power, & Wimbush (1992) cited a series of works in which they were characterized as being weak, disorganized, and vulnerable. The authors argued that views such as these have rarely been grounded in sound empirical research with controls for critical family characteristics such as parents' income or education.

A recent study in which potential confounds were addressed showed that after considering household income, minority parents were no more likely than Caucasians to display various punitive parenting behaviors such as those involving yelling, slapping, or spanking (Hashima & Amato, 1994). On the other hand, as compared to Caucasians, African American and Hispanic parents did report lower levels of supportive parenting behaviors such as praising or hugging, even after controlling for income. Explanations rested on the possibility of greater social desirability bias in reporting such behaviors among Caucasian parents, and of potentially unique stressors linked with minority status among the other groups. As noted later in this chapter, however, several investigators have reported contrary findings, showing that minority parents evidence more *positive* outcomes than Caucasians once levels of family income are taken into account.

Greater Risk Among Minority Children

Minority children in poverty fare more poorly than Caucasians in two domains, academic performance and externalizing problems, with their relative disadvantage in both domains increasing over time. Although the standardized test scores of African American students are typically close to those of Anglo-Americans when they begin school, a gap begins to appear almost immediately and often reaches two full grade levels by the sixth grade (see Steele, 1997, for a review). By high school, poor minority youth are often more vulnerable than their White counterparts to dropping out, with Hispanics being at even greater risk than African American students (Chavez, Oetting, & Swaim, 1994; Ripple & Luthar, 1998).

Whereas ethnic differences in achievement may be viewed as reflecting underlying genetic differences in intelligence (Herrnstein & Murray, 1994), variations in abilities do not, in themselves, seem to adequately account for differences in performance. Based on his research with various inner-city samples, for example, Ginsburg (1986) concluded that poor children, Blacks as well as Whites, did possess fundamental competencies in early mathematical thinking and displayed little evidence of pervasive cognitive deficit. Further, as Steele (1997) has noted, even when minority and Caucasian youth have comparable scores on standardized tests such as the Scholastic Assessment Test (SAT), the subsequent performance of minority students tends to fall far short of what would have been predicted by their abilities as indexed by their SAT scores.

Environmental forces that might inhibit minority students' achievement include frequently coexisting poverty status, as well as attitudes both within minority groups, and toward them, by larger society. Socioeconomic deprivation can impair school performance by limiting resources to support school persistence, both within schools and within families (National Research

Council, 1993). Beyond disadvantage, various cultural patterns can further attenuate minority students' academic motivation. Many of these youngsters are unconvinced that success at school will lead to success in later life due to their ongoing experiences with racism and marginalization, and perceptions of "job ceilings" which deny them access to prestigious jobs (see Arroyo & Zigler, 1995; Fordham & Ogbu, 1986; Ogbu, 1991; Spencer et al., 1993). Even among those minority students who *do* invest in school, exposure to negative stereotypes about their scholastic abilities tends to trigger high anxiety, which in turn can jeopardize the levels of academic success they are able to achieve (Steele, 1997).

Environmental forces are also implicated in the risks for externalizing problems, such as delinquency, among minority children. Among African American children more so than their Caucasian counterparts, male joblessness in the neighborhood has been found to be linked with increased risk for externalizing behavior problems (Chase-Lansdale & Gordon, 1996). Drawing upon Wilson's (1991) writings on social isolation, authors of this study reasoned that in inner-city neighborhoods with high male joblessness—areas in which African Americans are disproportionately represented—the dearth of role models of disciplined behaviors, which accompany regular adult employment, can significantly exacerbate behavior problems among African American youth.

Similar suggestions involving social structures have been offered in explaining findings that academic failure can increase risk for subsequent delinquency among Black youth more so than among Whites (Lynam et al., 1993). When African American boys become frustrated with school as a result of academic failure, they often remove themselves from its social control and thus become vulnerable to alternative social influences: often those of delinquents in the unstable, socially isolated neighborhoods in which Blacks are over-represented (Wilson, 1987).

Neighborhood influences can also be particularly pernicious for growth in crime involvement among minority youth. Ethnographic research has shown that as compared to Whites, minority teens show greater involvement in crime over time, as well as less cautiousness in ongoing criminal activities (Sullivan, 1996). Controls and resources in the adolescents' social and physical environments each appear to contribute to these differences. For example, households in Caucasian communities tend to have stronger labor market networks through which local youth can obtain jobs, as well as more adult males who exercise control of neighborhood streets (e.g., by directly disciplining delinquent youth or by working with the local police precinct) (Sullivan, 1996).

Ethnic Minority Subgroups at Special Risk:
Hispanic Families

Whereas poor families from different minority groups share many adversities, they also, obviously, have several unique experiences. Existing research shows that in terms of "overall" vulnerability reflected by a minority subgroup, risks among Hispanic parents and children are particularly high.[3] As compared to their low-SES African American counterparts, Hispanic mothers tend to have lower levels of social support and more restrictive childrearing attitudes (Wasserman et al., 1990). The lower vulnerability of African American mothers may reflect, in part, relatively high support from extended kin. On the other hand, the greater vulnerability of the Hispanic mothers can arise from exposure to several unique stressors related to migration, acculturation, difficulties with language, and social isolation (Canino, Gould, Prupis, & Shafer, 1986; Sanders-Phillips, Moisan, Wadlington, Morgan, & English, 1995).

Differences among Hispanic mothers have also been identified: relatively recent immigrants appear to reflect greater difficulties in their roles as parents (e.g., in terms of levels of aggravation or strictness as parents) as compared to longer term U.S. residents (Wasserman et al., 1990). As Garcia Coll and Vasquez Garcia (1995) noted, new Hispanic immigrants to the U.S. must acculturate not only to an alien culture and language but also, frequently, to urban poverty at the same time. Clearly, these challenges can complicate the adjustment process for both parents and children.

Like their parents, Latino children also have been found to show more difficulties than Blacks, with differences documented across diverse domains including depressive symptoms, problems at school, and substance use (e.g., Bettes, Dusenbury, Kerner, James-Ortiz, & Botvin, 1990; Jessor et al., 1995; Ripple & Luthar, 1998; Sanders-Phillips et al., 1995). Apart from problems related to acculturation (e.g., limited access to informal peer support at school), such findings have been viewed as possibly reflecting various cultural-familial factors. It has been argued, for example, that Latino children are particularly prone to guilt when they do not live up to parental expectations, and that they experience conflict in negotiating two value systems— that of the family which emphasizes respect and obedience, and that in the Anglo world which encourages individuation and separation (see Florsheim, Tolan, & Gorman-Smith, 1996; Sanders-Phillips et al., 1995).

The African American Male

Whereas African American youth generally reflect less vulnerability than their Hispanic counterparts, *among* Black youth living in poverty, boys are at higher risk than girls (see Hammond & Yung, 1993; Spencer, 1995). Their greater vulnerability is perhaps most starkly reflected in statistics on death by firearms. National statistics indicate that during 1992, such deaths (including homicides, suicides, and unintentional deaths) were recorded for over 150 African American males between 10 and 19 years of age (Christoffel, 1997). Rates for White males, Black females, and White females were 33.3, 16.3, and 5.7, respectively.

In the realms of academic performance and subsequent employment, Black boys fare more poorly than girls across the developmental span. Research reviews have indicated that as compared to females, African American males perform at significantly lower levels during elementary and secondary school as well as in higher education. In addition, African American males are at special risk for chronic joblessness and discouragement in seeking employment following the high school years (Bowman, 1990).

In an intriguing analysis, Seitz and Apfel (1997) suggested that the greater vulnerability among African American boys may be reflected not just in their own lives but also those of their mothers. The authors demonstrated that as compared to teen mothers whose firstborns were girls, those with firstborn sons were far less able to avoid welfare dependency. They were also less likely to delay subsequent childbearing, and to be married in the 12 years after their child was born, possibly reflecting perceptions (often accurate) among both the mothers and their potential husbands, of young male children being at greater risk for long-term problems than females in the ecological context of urban poverty.

Apart from the adverse environmental forces that affect minority children in general (see preceding section), several additional factors can exacerbate the problems of African Americans boys. Spencer (1995) has argued, for example, that Black boys tend to physically mature earlier and to be heavier and taller than their Caucasian counterparts. As a result of their earlier maturity, as well as widespread societal stereotypes, these boys may often be perceived as threatening by people in their environments who consequently offer them less support and convey views of them as fitting profiles for expected deviance. "(An) early-maturing, 10-year-old, black, male, inner-city youth may not be viewed, assisted, and interacted with like a child in need of support. The experience too often for these children is an awareness of being perceived as a frightening black man" (Spencer, 1995; p. 54).

With SES Controlled, African American Families May Fare Better Than Caucasians

Contradicting the notion that minority group adults inevitably show more psychopathology than Caucasians, there is some evidence that within the same SES levels, African Americans sometimes reflect equivalent or even lower levels of risk. Epidemiological data from the National Comorbidity Survey (NCS; Kessler et al., 1994), for example, indicated that there were no disorders on which Black adults had higher rates—either lifetime or active prevalence—than Whites. Furthermore, Blacks had significantly lower rates than Whites on affective disorders, substance use disorders, as well as lifetime comorbidity (two or more co-occurring psychiatric disorders).[4]

Advantages of Blacks over Whites are also evident in studies of disadvantaged teenage parents. Hetherington (1997) has noted that although African American adolescents are more likely than Caucasians to become teen parents, outcomes for them appear to be less adverse. Black teen parents are more likely than Whites to receive kin support with child care, for example, and are less likely to be seen as culturally deviant. Additionally, differences in disadvantage between teenage and older mothers are typically lower among Blacks than Whites, and single African American fathers maintain more contact with their children, an advantage that is reflected, in turn, in more positive outcomes among their children.

Relative advantages in specific parenting behaviors have been documented as well. As compared to their Caucasian counterparts, African American parents in high-crime neighborhoods have been found to use a stronger normative context against substance use by their teen children. They appear to perceive alcohol use as more harmful, have stronger rules against adolescent substance use, and involve their children less in adult use of alcohol (Peterson, Hawkins, Abbott, & Catalano, 1994).

Paralleling trends documented among adults, minority children do not necessarily reflect greater vulnerability than Caucasians of the same socioeconomic status (Dodge et al., 1994; Seidman, Allen, Aber, Mitchell, & Feinman, 1994). Epidemiological data from the Great Smoky Mountains Study, based on 4,500 youth between 9 and 13 years of age, indicated that African American youth did not show greater psychopathology than Caucasians after poverty and rural/urban residence were considered (Costello, et al., 1996).

Rather than simply showing that minority children can be comparable to Whites with family background held constant, some have found that they actually might be at an advantage. For example, comparisons of American Indian (Cherokee) and White children in the Great Smoky Mountains epidemiological study indicated significant links between family poverty and child psychiatric diagnoses among the latter but not the former, suggesting that American Indian children may have been protected more so than Whites against the ill-effects of poverty (Costello, Farmer, Angold, Burns, & Erkanli, 1997). Similarly, several investigators have reported that within low-SES groups, African American youth can fare better than their Caucasian peers in terms of mental health indices as well as socially competent behaviors in everyday life (Baldwin et al., 1993; Fabrega, Ulrich, & Loeber, 1996; Luthar, Cushing, Merikangas, & Rounsaville, 1998).

A compendium of recent studies points to various material, social, and protective factors that might buffer Black parents and children against mental health problems (see Neighbors & Jackson, 1996). There is much evidence, for example, of the significance of both kin and non-kin sources of support in helping these individuals cope with stressors (Chapter 5). It has also been suggested that African Americans may be more likely than others to use constructive coping strategies (such as confronting problems or seeking informal help), rather than escapist strategies such as drinking or taking drugs, which are often linked with high levels of distress (Broman, 1996).

Other interpretations of better mental health among disadvantaged Blacks than Caucasians have rested on sociocultural forces. Baldwin and colleagues have argued, for example, that minority groups, having had a long history of disadvantage in this country, may have developed more effective ways of coping with chronic deprivation over the years. Alternatively, social comparison forces may be at work so that the negative connotations of living in poverty may be felt more keenly by Whites than Blacks, for whom there is a greater precedent of others living in similar circumstances (Baldwin et al., 1993; Luthar et al., 1998).

Intriguing perspectives on minority youth's mental health are presented by Steele (1997), who has argued that the self-regard of these youngsters often rests less on success in domains valued by mainstream society (such as academics), and more on other areas which involve low threats of being negatively stereotyped. In his review paper, Steele cited a series of studies to show that although Black students typically perform less well academically than Whites, their global self-esteem is typically as high as, or higher than, that of Whites. Based on these dual threads of evidence, he reasoned that Black students tend to be relatively impervious to failures in domains where they view their evaluative prospects as being poor, such as academic achievement. At the same time, their overall self-regard can be bolstered substantially by identification with domains that carry better prospects, such as success in the peer group.

Although various factors may in fact result in less distress among poor African American individuals than Caucasians, findings in this regard must be viewed with considerable caution for at least two reasons. First, ratings of adjustment are by no means absolute indicators of psychological health, but are inevitably tied to norms within a particular reference group (Weisz et al.,

1997). Thus, while many poor Black individuals may not rate their own life circumstances and mental health as highly deviant in comparison to others disenfranchised like themselves, this does not necessarily indicate low distress in any absolute terms. Second, findings of advantages in some domains of adjustment must not obscure evidence of the difficulties that remain in several areas among poor African American youth, particularly boys, including substantial disadvantages in the realms of neighborhood influences, schooling, and ultimately, access to gainful employment in mainstream society.

SUMMARY

1. Teenage mothers are overrepresented among the poor. As compared to older mothers, they are at greater risk for negative parenting behaviors, although the magnitude of differences is attenuated when other characteristics (such as income level, marital status, and contextual factors) are considered. By contrast, *children* of teen mothers more consistently display vulnerability to negative outcomes, even after considering such background variables.

2. Single-parent household status (most often in reality, mother-headed household status) exacerbates the already high risks faced by children who live in poverty. At the same time, some recent findings indicate the need for more careful consideration of ways in which poor fathers who do not live with their children do or could contribute, to their children's well-being.

Co-residence with grandparents (common among single, disadvantaged mothers) can serve several protective functions, but can also sometimes exacerbate difficulties, e.g., by increasing conflicts among adults living in close physical proximity and by adding to the burdens placed on grandparents' resources.

3. The socializing goals of parents can vary greatly depending on their ethnic group membership. It has also been suggested that the ramifications of particular parenting behaviors can vary across different ethnic groups, wherein high parental strictness and control, for example, are conducive for African American children in poverty but detrimental for Caucasians. Further research is needed to establish the degree to which findings such as these reflect ethnic differences in developmental processes as opposed to differences in related determinants (e.g., the typically higher levels of neighborhood

violence and disorganization which comprise the immediate socializing context for poor Black families more so than Whites).

4. Minority group families experience poverty more frequently and in a more severe and persistent form than do Whites. These adversities, along with other stressors related to discrimination, negative stereotyping, and living in resource-poor neighborhoods, are starkly reflected in the substantial disadvantage of minority children in areas of school-based competence and externalizing behaviors.

5. All ethnic minorities are not at comparable risk. Hispanic youth and their parents collectively display greater vulnerability than their Black counterparts in poverty, reflecting several unique stressors such as those linked with migration and acculturation. Among African American youth, similarly, boys fare more poorly than girls across several domains, reflecting once again, the confluence of unique risks they experience related to biological as well as contextual, sociocultural factors.

6. On some mental health indices such as global self-esteem, African American children, as well as their parents, may fare better than Caucasians *once variations in income levels are taken into account.* Trends such as these may reflect protective forces among Blacks, such as high kin support and the use of relatively constructive coping strategies. Despite their strengths in some domains, however, there are many spheres of life in which poor African American children and their parents continue to experience substantial challenges.

Notably, there is little parallel evidence to date of poor Hispanic parents or children being at an advantage over Caucasians: there is little question that these individuals comprise a subgroup contending with inordinate adversities. The multiple strains induced by poverty concomitant with the task of adjusting to an alien culture, call for concerted attention to the unique psychological needs of immigrant parents and children who must contend with conditions of serious socioeconomic disadvantage.

NOTES

1. Most research on teen parents has been focused on teen mothers, who are more likely than fathers to remain involved in raising the child. For research on teen fathers, see Lerman and Ooms (1993).

2. The national poverty threshold is an index that was originally calculated based on the estimated cost of a very basic diet of food, multiplied by three. The figure is adjusted annually

for inflation and family size, but not for geographic region or non-cash benefits (Huston et al., 1994).

3. Existing research on social-emotional adjustment of minority children in poverty has been focused largely on African American and Hispanic youth; there is currently little evidence on adaptation patterns among other ethnic minorities in disadvantaged circumstances (e.g., Asian Americans or Native Americans).

4. While noting methodological differences between the NCS and the previously cited Kessler and Neighbors (1986) study, the authors also raised the possibility that some incompletely understood resources might protect minority group individuals from the adverse effects of their stressful life circumstances (Kessler et al., 1994).

4

POVERTY AND THE FAMILY

Psychological Processes

She stands with her hands on her hips. She wears shorts and a Red Sox T-shirt, bare thick arms. She is grass-stained, soggy, and bruised from hard play. She says huskily, "Ma, it's worse in here." In one hand is a single black-eyed Susan.

The room is near ninety degrees. Houseflies wheel against the ceiling. Earlene turns her head away from the light of the open door so that it only touches the outline of her razorlike cheekbone.

Bonny Loo goes to the foot of the bed and squeezes her mother's toes. "Feel that, Ma?" she asks.

Earlene nods.

"You ain't dead yet, then!" the child chirps.

Earlene closes her eyes.

Bonny Loo waves the black-eyed Susan in her mother's face. "Actually, these kinda flowers stink," she says.

Earlene's large eyes have begun to sink. The mouth looks huge.

Bonny Loo says, "Gramp's called the hospital about you. You're goin' there."

Bonny Loo sits on the bed. "It's awful in here, Ma!"

Earlene says, "It's okay. It's quiet."

"Ain't quiet," says Bonny Loo, glaring at the wheeling flies. Bonny Loo's shoulders suddenly stoop. She stretches her T-shirt up to wipe her face. She makes a little animal grunt and her face goes red. She sobs and her eyes are lost in tears.

—Chute, 1985, *The Beans of Egypt,* Maine, pp. 146-147

The well-being of every child is intricately tied in with the functioning of his or her parents, and when socioeconomic resources are unremittingly scant, the challenges of daily living can substantially erode parents' mental health. Vicissitudes in their caregivers' psychological adaptation, in turn, are reflected in problems in the children's own adjustment across various spheres of social-emotional development.

Psychological processes involved in the adjustment of parents and children in poverty comprise the focus of this chapter, with relevant research findings presented in three broad sections. The first is focused on aspects of poor parents' own adaptation, including dimensions of serious psychopathology, personal attributes, and exposure to life stressors. The second section concerns specific parenting behaviors: ways in which parents interact with their children including behaviors pertaining to discipline or monitoring, and those on the warmth-rejection continuum. In each of these two sections, discussions generally focus first on the effects of poverty on particular facets of parents' adaptation, and next, on the effects of that parental construct, in turn, on children's adjustment profiles. Major conceptual models of family functioning in the context of poverty are discussed in the final section of this chapter.

POVERTY AND PARENTS' FUNCTIONING

Parental Psychopathology

Research on disadvantaged parents' psychopathology has typically been focused on mothers, with fathers ill-represented, and much of the extant research has addressed problems of depression and of substance abuse. High levels of depressive symptoms have been documented among poor mothers during the phases of pregnancy, as well as their children's early childhood years (Alpern & Lyons-Ruth, 1993; Reis et al., 1986). Among low-income Hispanic and African American women who had recently given birth to a child, Wasserman et al. (1990) reported that between 60% and 70% of the mothers reported clinically significant levels of depressive symptoms. In other research, rates of clinically significant depression have been found to be twice as high among inner-city pregnant and postpartum women as compared to middle-class samples (Hobfoll, Ritter, Lavin, Hulsizer, & Cameron, 1995).

Depressive feelings can adversely affect various aspects of parenting behavior. Literature reviews on maternal depression (e.g., Cummings & Davies, 1994; Cicchetti & Toth, 1995) have indicated, for example, that depressed mothers tend to be less attentive than others to their children, alternate between disengagement and intrusiveness, show lower reciprocity and synchronicity. They also tend to express more negative affect, make more negative attributions about their children, and are at risk for hostile, coercive parenting as well as child maltreatment.

Whereas processes such as these may occur among depressed women in general, the effects of maternal depression on parenting can be particularly pronounced among impoverished families. To illustrate, disadvantaged mothers experiencing high personal distress tend to reflect low supportiveness and high aversiveness in their parenting behaviors—regardless of their children's behavior problems (Dumas & Wekerle, 1995). By contrast, among less disadvantaged mothers, parenting behaviors appear to be influenced more by mothers' perceptions of behavior problems in children, rather than their personal distress levels. Such findings suggest that in comparison with cues reflected in specific child behaviors, the acute personal distress and life stress experienced by chronically disadvantaged mothers can be far more potent in affecting the ways in which they interact with young children in their care.

Maternal depression can affect poor children via disturbances across various facets of mothers' behaviors, both negative and positive. To illustrate, among inner-city, adolescent mothers, maternal depressive symptoms during the first year postpartum appeared to affect subsequent behavior problems in children only partially—not entirely—via the mediating route of escalated mother-child conflict (Leadbeater et al., 1996). In another study involving preschoolers, the intervening variable of the quality of children's attachments with mothers (as captured by attachment representations) only partially explained the links found between levels of maternal depression, and children's subsequent behavior problems (Hubbs-Tait et al., 1996).

Abuse of illicit drugs is another form of parental psychopathology to which many children living in poverty can be vulnerable (Klerman, 1994), and research in this domain has been focused, again, largely on affected mothers rather than fathers (Luthar et al., 1997). Drug abusing mothers exhibit a range of problems in their parenting (for reviews, see Luthar & Suchman, in press; Mayes & Bornstein, 1997). As compared to substance-free parents, for example, these mothers respond to their babies' cues less frequently and make fewer attempts to elicit communications from them, and with their older children, often use authoritarian disciplinary approaches which reinforce negative attention-seeking behaviors.

Parental substance abuse is also linked with elevated risk for child maltreatment (Mayes & Bornstein, 1997; Murphy et al., 1991). Based on their examination of multiple demographic and psychiatric indices in relation to child maltreatment, Chaffin, Kelleher, and Hollenberg (1996) found that parents' substance abuse almost tripled the risk of both child abuse and neglect. By contrast, other research has suggested that when multiple demographic and psychiatric indices are considered, parental drug abuse *per se* is linked with heightened risk for child neglect, but not of child abuse (Egami, Ford, Greenfield, & Crum, 1996).

As might be expected, children of addicted parents reflect vulnerability to negative outcomes, with problems going beyond those resulting from poverty alone. Comparisons of school-age offspring of substance abusing mothers, with children of nonaddicted mothers of the same SES, have indicated significantly higher problems among the former across multiple areas of symptomatology (deCubas and Field, 1993).

The problems of substance abusers' children also appear to escalate the longer they live with an addicted parent. Prenatal exposure to drugs is potentially, though not inevitably, linked with developmental problems at birth and during early infancy (see Hawley & Disney, 1992; Mayes & Bornstein, 1997). By contrast, older children living with addicted parents reflect a range of problems (Azuma & Chasnoff, 1992; Wilens, Biederman, Kiely, Bredin, & Spencer, 1995). By the early adolescent years, as many as 60% have been found to have at least one lifetime diagnosis of psychiatric disorder (Luthar et al., 1998).

Although drug abusing mothers are typically viewed as uncaring if not deliberately callous parents, many addicted mothers are deeply concerned about their children and are strongly invested in improving their life circumstances (Luthar & Suchman, in press). Addicted mothers are neither unaware of, nor sanguine about, their difficulties around parenting. To the contrary, studies have shown that they can be highly responsive to parenting interventions which (1) acknowledge the intensity of their maternal emotions of guilt and confusion, as well as concern and protectiveness, (2) are based in respect and supportiveness, and (3) consider the potency of life circumstances that would drain any parent's resources (e.g., social isolation, depression, and exposure to physical and sexual abuse) (Luthar & Suchman, in press; Zuckerman, 1994). Far from supporting notions of drug abusing mothers as irredeemably inimical parents, therefore, current evidence underscores the need for concerted efforts to provide more thoughtful interventions for these highly vulnerable, yet underserved parents—for their own welfare as well as for the scores of young children for whose care they are often solely responsible.

Parents' Developmental History
and Personal Resources

Developmental history. Individuals' development histories are critical for their functioning as parents (Belsky, 1980; 1984), and research has shown that the quality of disadvantaged mothers' childhood relationships with their own mothers can affect the quality of their parenting as adults (Lyons-Ruth, Zoll, Connell, & Grunebaum, 1989). Observational assessments of African American families have revealed significant links between the quality of the mother-grandmother relationship and contemporaneous maternal parenting (Wakschlag, Chase-Lansdale, & Brooks-Gunn,1996). Mothers whose inter-actions with their own mothers were characterized by an autonomous and flexible style tended to display such positive parenting behaviors with their own children, even after considering maternal age and personal resources (e.g., intelligence and maturity indices), as well as other aspects of the mother-grandmother relationship such as emotional closeness. These find-ings were interpreted from a relational perspective, where individuation was viewed as the capacity to balance autonomy and connectedness which reflected stability across different relationships intergenerationally (Wakschlag et al., 1996). The converse of such assertions is, of course, equally likely: In the absence of "corrective" interpersonal experiences—e.g., exposure to supportive interventions or marriage to a supportive spouse (Luthar & Suchman, in press; Rutter, 1990)—disadvantaged mothers who themselves were seriously deprived of adult nurturance as children are likely to show difficulties in these areas as they come to parent the next generation.

Positive attributes and personal resources. Research on parents in poverty has focused disproportionately on aspects of maladjustment, with less atten-tion to positive parental characteristics. Research by Emory Cowen and his colleagues (Cowen et al., 1997) attests to the protective value, for disadvan-taged children, of their parents' *psychological well-being,* as indexed by domains such as sense of parenting efficacy, overall life satisfaction, and optimistic views of the child's future. Similarly, among daughters of highly stressed mothers, levels of social-emotional competence have been found to be related to *positive maternal social and problem-solving characteristics* (Pianta, Egeland, & Sroufe, 1990), possibly reflecting buffering effects of mothers' psychological health for girls, as well as the benefits of adaptive role models. There is also evidence of protective effects associated with mothers' *internal locus of control* as well as high levels of *self-esteem* (Luster & McAdoo, 1994; Stevens, 1988).

Whereas *maternal intelligence* typically shows positive links with disadvantaged children's IQ scores and achievement levels, its role in their social-emotional functioning is less clear. In research with African American families, robust links have been identified between maternal intelligence and children's achievement scores (Luster & McAdoo, 1994). By contrast, mothers' IQ was unrelated to children's behavior problems, after other maternal characteristics, such as self-esteem and age at first birth, were considered.

In recent research involving disadvantaged, drug abusing mothers, maternal receptive vocabulary scores, typically highly correlated with IQ (Dunn & Dunn, 1981), were found to be *negatively* linked with children's psychosocial adjustment as measured by their everyday social competence as well as disruptive behavior diagnoses (Luthar et al., 1998). These trends were more marked among African Americans than Caucasians. Given that receptive vocabulary scores are influenced by individuals' educational levels, the authors suggested that the African American mothers with high scores may have had more privileged backgrounds than others. Furthermore, drug addiction among this subgroup may have reflected greater psychopathology among the mothers, greater censure from their upwardly mobile families, and/or simply more feelings of personal failure; problems which could each, in turn, have affected the psychological adaptation of children in their care.

Trends such as these might also, however, reflect specific parenting predilections among intelligent individuals. In epidemiological research involving eleven 13-year-old children, high *child* intelligence was found to be protective in terms of child psychopathology; yet, high *parental* intelligence was linked with greater child symptomatology, as indexed by both parents' and school reports (Goodman, Simonoff, & Stevenson, 1995). Authors of this work suggested that bright parents may often exert excessive pressure on children to succeed intellectually and academically, and/or that parents' IQ might be linked with other aspects of parenting such as overprotectiveness, which engender greater maladjustment in the child. In sum, a range of processes have been suggested, though none conclusively established, as possibly underlying links between high levels of parental intelligence and greater risk for child maladjustment in some domains.

Stressful life experiences. Low-income parents are vulnerable to a range of stressful life experiences which exacerbate their mental health difficulties. For example, mothers living in poverty are victims of physical and sexual violence with alarming frequency. In a study by Browne and Bassuk (1997), 61% reported severe violence by a male partner. Interpersonal stressors such as these and others (e.g., related to health problems and financial instability) may often exacerbate mothers' depressive symptoms over time, and high maternal distress in turn can increase the risk of mothers' exposure to further stressful experiences (Pianta & Egeland, 1994).

Negative life experiences also affect the quality of care that disadvantaged parents are able to provide to their children. Mothers who experience high stress in their personal relationships tend to demonstrate more intrusive and insensitive parenting styles in interactions with their infants (Pianta & Egeland, 1990). Similarly, women who are neglectful toward their children typically report a surfeit of life stressors including those linked with marital disruptions, having to care for several young children in the home, and restricted access to material resources for child care (Giovannoni & Billingsley, 1970).

Parallel to trends observed among their parents, studies with disadvantaged children have also indicated relatively frequent exposure to negative life events, which in turn can exacerbate risk for adjustment problems (Luthar, 1991). Among school-age youth, frequent negative life events in the family (e.g., having little food to eat and involvement in serious family arguments) can be linked with attenuated engagement at school (e.g., Wyman et al., 1993). Similarly, youngsters who perceive their own lives as highly stressful are significantly more likely than others to exhibit adjustment difficulties across multiple behavioral and social competence dimensions (Smith & Prior, 1995).

Frequent daily hassles also exacerbate risks for adjustment problems (Allen, Denner, Yoshikawa, Seidman, & Aber, 1996), with effects possibly more pronounced among poor youth than others. Prospective research involving early adolescents has shown that frequent everyday hassles are related to subsequent adaptational problems among disadvantaged youth as well as their nondisadvantaged counterparts. However, the strength of these associations appears to be substantially larger among the former (DuBois et al., 1994; see also Attar, Guerra, & Tolan, 1994), suggesting the likely erosion of environmental and personal resources for negotiating everyday hassles among children in poor families, more so than among their more privileged peers.

PARENTAL BEHAVIORS

Discipline and Limit-Setting

Whereas controversy remains about whether the implications of parental strictness might vary by ethnicity (Chapter 3), there is broad consensus that consistent parental monitoring is generally beneficial for children living in dangerous neighborhoods. A wealth of evidence, gleaned from both quantitative and qualitative research, confirms that the maintenance of structure and rules in the household, and high monitoring of children, reduce the likelihood of maladaptive behaviors among youth in low-income, delinquency-prone environments (Apfel & Seitz, 1997; Baldwin, Baldwin, & Cole, 1990; Haapasalo & Tremblay, 1994; Jarrett, 1995; Luster & McAdoo, 1996; McLoyd, 1990; Simon & Burns, 1997; Werner & Smith, 1992); some representative findings are briefly reviewed.

Long-term benefits of parental supervision are evident in findings on children's predilections to aggressive behaviors. Among low-SES boys who consistently displayed low levels of physical aggression between the ages of 6 and 12 years, Haapasalo and Tremblay (1994) reported that a distinctive characteristic was high levels of parental supervision. More so than their aggressive counterparts, these "non-fighters" indicated that their parents were constantly aware of where, and with whom they spent their free time through the period spanning their preadolescent years.

Parallel findings have been obtained in relation to other adjustment outcomes. As noted previously, positive school performance among inner-city youth tends to be linked with restrictive, authoritarian parenting behaviors rather than democratic ones (among more mainstream teens, by contrast, high parental control has more negative connotations) (Baldwin et al., 1990; Gonzales, Cauce, Friedman, & Mason, in press). Protective effects have also been found for proactive parenting practices in relation to children's levels of substance use. Adolescents' risk for alcohol use tends to be lower when parents regularly monitor their activities and set clear expectations for their behaviors (Peterson et al., 1994). Collectively, then, extant evidence indicates that parental supervision can be critical in shielding inner-city youth from temptations to engage in maladaptive behaviors widespread among peers in their communities, such as disavowal of school and indulgence in various antisocial, illegal, and ultimately, self-destructive pursuits.

Warmth and Support

Parental behaviors reflecting high warmth and support can substantially reduce the risks associated with poverty (Smith & Prior, 1995). Children whose mothers provide responsive, supportive, and structured, home environments during their early childhood years tend to display relatively high levels of competence subsequently, as elementary school students (Pianta et al., 1990). Based on 5- and 10-year follow-up data on a disadvantaged cohort recruited at birth, Osborn (1990) identified a subgroup of children who showed relatively high cognitive and behavioral competence. The overriding familial protective factor distinguishing these youth from others was child-centered and supportive parenting. Similarly, data from the Rochester Child Resilience Project (Cowen et al., 1997) have shown that among inner-city elementary school children experiencing high life stress, a sound parent-child relationship—characterized by features such as continuity, nurturance, and consistent discipline—was significantly linked with positive versus negative child outcomes.

Supportive relationships with parents also afford disadvantaged youth with protection from the challenges of adolescent development. Among early adolescents, the benefits of high family support can be evident in reduced levels of both psychological distress and conduct problems over time (DuBois et al., 1994). In a similar vein, the likelihood of positive educational outcomes among African American teens has been found to be more strongly linked with perceptions of family support than with economic status of their families, or with conditions in their neighborhoods (Connell et al., 1994; 1995).

As compared to support from family members, the implications of a more global index of family functioning, *family cohesion*, seem to be more equivocal among inner-city youth. Some investigators have found positive links between adolescents' perceptions of family cohesion and their adjustment across diverse indices (e.g., Felner, Aber, Primavera, & Cauce, 1985). Conversely, two recent studies have yielded contrasting trends depending on gender, with one reflecting protective effects of family cohesion for boys but negative ones for girls (Weist, et al., 1995), and the other suggesting salutary effects for girls but not boys (Juarez et al., 1997). Such inconsistencies in findings may reflect unreliability of measurement or the possibility that at high levels, family cohesion might border on enmeshment from the perspective of some subgroups of adolescents (Juarez et al., 1997).

Contradictions are also evident within the scant evidence that is currently available on the role of disadvantaged fathers' involvement with their children. Among preschool children of teen mothers, externalizing problems have been found to be *lower* when fathers remained relatively uninvolved, as opposed to highly involved with their care (by contributing materially, or living with or visiting the child) (Leadbeater, Way, & Raden, 1996). These findings may reflect elevated conflict between highly involved fathers and mothers, deriving, for example, from disagreements about disciplinary practices for their young children (Shaw, Owens, Vondra, Keenan, & Winslow, 1996). Additionally, some young children of highly involved fathers in poverty may be exposed to high levels of paternal problem behaviors such as those relating to substance abuse or depression (Leadbeater et al., 1996). Contrasting with these results with preschoolers are findings of a strong protective role of paternal support for adolescents. In a study involving African American teenage boys, the level of emotional support received from the father, and time spent with him, were each linked with various indices of adolescents' well-being, regardless of whether or not fathers lived in the same household as their children (Zimmerman et al., 1995; see also Furstenberg & Harris, 1993). Conjointly, therefore, available data suggest that when children in poverty are still young, the active involvement of non-coresiding fathers can sometimes escalate difficulties for children (e.g., when there is overt rancor between the father and the primary caregiver, the mother). However, if these fathers remain in close touch with their children during the adolescent years, they may often serve as a source of substantial support for their children's social-emotional development across multiple spheres of adaptation.

Maltreatment

Poverty and Child Maltreatment. Although child maltreatment occurs across the socioeconomic spectrum, it is disproportionately reported among disadvantaged families (Cicchetti & Lynch, 1995; Eckenrode et al., 1995; Trickett, Aber, Carlson, & Cicchetti, 1991). Various stresses linked with parents' poverty can escalate risks for child maltreatment including feelings of frustration and powerlessness as a result of unemployment, limited funds for child care, isolation from formal and informal support systems, and chronic exposure to violence in communities (Belsky, 1980; Cicchetti & Lynch, 1995).

Whereas low SES and maltreatment can have independent, negative effects on children's development (see Cicchetti & Lynch, 1995), epidemiological data suggest that the effects of poverty on child maltreatment may not be as strong as those of parental psychopathology. Based on almost 10,000 respondents in the Epidemiological Catchment Area (ECA) Study, Egami and colleagues (1996) reported that when parents' sociodemographic characteristics and their psychiatric diagnoses were collectively considered in relation to child maltreatment, effects of SES were not statistically significant. On the other hand, when sociodemographics were held constant in statistical analyses, parents' psychopathology indices retained significant links with child abuse as well as neglect. Similar trends, indicating stronger unique effects for parental psychopathology than for family poverty, were reported in other analyses of two waves of data from the ECA Survey (Chaffin et al., 1996).

Maltreatment and Child Outcomes. Early exposure to maltreatment constrains the resolution of early developmental tasks, and consequently, paves the way for later developmental deviations (Cicchetti & Lynch, 1995; Egeland et al., 1993). Consonant with these organizational perspectives, differences between low-income children who are maltreated, and those who are not, have been found to escalate over time (Crittenden, 1985; Egeland & Sroufe, 1981). Egeland and Sroufe (1981) found that infants of psychologically unavailable low-income mothers showed sharp declines across time and across diverse domains, including quality of attachment and participation in both feeding and play situations. By 24 months, these children were described as easily frustrated, noncompliant, and angry. During the preschool years, they displayed more emotional and behavioral problems than comparison children and by the school years, many showed signs of serious psychopathology (Egeland et al., 1993). Findings such as these testify to the urgent need for prevention efforts, targeting disenfranchised women at high risk for subsequent maltreatment during their pregnancies and their children's early infancies, rather than intervening with remedial or punitive measures (such as revocation of parental rights) only after problems have become well-entrenched.

Even at older ages, disadvantaged children reflect considerable vulnerability to maltreatment and violence within the family. Among African American preadolescents and adolescents living around public housing developments, intra-familial violence indices, such as corporal punishment and conflict in the family, were shown to be related to concurrent measurements of self-reported depression and hopelessness (DuRant, Getts, Cadenhead, Emans, & Woods, 1995). Moreover, these indices had stronger links with measures of children's psychological distress than did levels of neighborhood violence.

Among the mechanisms that underlie links between maltreatment and child maladjustment, critical are disturbances in affective and cognitive processes (see Cicchetti & Lynch, 1995, for a review). Early parent-child interactions are important in shaping children's capacity to control emotional arousal, and maltreatment can lead to difficulties in regulating affect and accurately interpreting others' emotional reactions, which in turn, lead children to respond to experiences in ways that foster maladjustment. Also frequently implicated are disturbances in the quality of attachments developed with primary caregivers, which then form a template for many other interpersonal relationships within the child's life. Exposure to maltreatment also affects the development of an autonomous self. Maltreated children often have negative feelings about themselves, for example, and are reluctant to talk about their negative emotional states, characteristics which impede their abilities to engage in successful interpersonal relationships. In sum, then, exposure to maltreatment sets into motion a probabilistic trajectory that is characterized by increased likelihood of failure on many stage-salient tasks of development, with problems of adjustment frequently becoming compounded over time across diverse areas of adaptation (Cicchetti & Lynch, 1995).

MODELS OF FAMILY FUNCTIONING IN THE CONTEXT OF POVERTY

Families as Mediators of the Effects of Poverty

Whereas diverse familial processes have been described individually up to this point, several studies, following Glen Elder's pioneering work on families during the Great Depression (Elder, 1974; Elder et al., 1985; see also McLoyd, 1990), have been focused on family functioning as *mediators* of the effects of poverty on child functioning. Put briefly, the thesis here is that associations between poverty and child adjustment are not direct but operate instead through the parents' mental health and their parenting behaviors, and these in turn, serve as proximal influences which directly impinge on the child.

During the last decade, investigations involving this model have encompassed relations between economic disadvantage and various aspects of parents' functioning including depressive affect, perceptions of the parental role, and quality of the marital relationship; as well as aspects of parenting behavior including both warmth and discipline or monitoring (e.g., Brody et al., 1994; Conger, Ge, Elder, Lorenz, & Simons, 1994; Dodge et al., 1994; Felner et al., 1995; McLoyd et al., 1994; Lempers et al., 1989; Sampson & Laub, 1994). Sample sizes in these studies have generally ranged between 100 and 500 families. With few exceptions (e.g., Sampson & Laub, 1994) child outcomes have been assessed in terms of cumulative externalizing or internalizing symptoms (as opposed to psychiatric diagnoses), and in some instances, levels of academic achievement.

Overall, results of this body of work has supported the proposed model, generally showing that parental characteristics seem to mediate at least some of the effects of poverty on children's adjustment. Beyond this broad conclusion, however, there are several other themes reflected by this collection of studies.

First, the models tested have typically explained only a modest proportion of the total variability in child outcomes (between 10% and 30%), with stronger effects for children's academic achievement and disruptive behavior problems than for internalizing ones, such as depressive symptomatology. Notable exceptions to this trend were findings by Sampson and Laub (1994), in which almost half of the variability in child outcomes was accounted for. The relatively high variance explained in this case may partly have resulted from the use of a large, heterogeneous sample. Sampson and Laub's report was based on Glueck and Glueck's (1950) study of 500 youth with serious psychopathology (persistent juvenile delinquency), and 500 who were relatively well-adjusted.

Second, disturbances in parents' emotional and behavioral adaptation account for some, but by no means all or even most, of the overall effects of family poverty on children's development (e.g., Dodge et al., 1994; Harnish, Harnish, Dodge, & Valente, 1995; Felner et al., 1995; Lempers et al., 1989). These findings evoke various inferences. The first is that poverty clearly affects children not only via parents' adjustment difficulties but also, substantially, through various extra-familial routes including problems within their schools, neighborhoods, and wider communities. Additionally, even within the realm of the family, there may be important dimensions that have been relatively neglected in prior mediation model studies. As discussed later in this chapter, for example, genetic factors may partially explain links between family poverty and child maladjustment. There may also be substantial explanatory power linked with positive parental attributes, such as ego strength, optimism, or overall feelings of competence (e.g., Brody et al., 1994; Cowen et al., 1997), as well as with "nonpsychological" (yet more fundamental) tasks that confront many poor parents, including the degree to which they can provide for their children's basic needs of food, shelter, and health care (see Jarrett, 1994).

Third, links between poverty, family functioning, and child adjustment can involve several bidirectional associations. For example, children might influence their parents, and parental distress may affect the family's socioeconomic status (Bolger et al., 1995; Harnish et al., 1995; Sampson & Laub, 1994). Finally, the available evidence suggests that the links are not necessarily specific to either parent's gender. Whereas Elder and colleagues (1985) found that economic hardship among families during the 1930s influenced paternal but not maternal behaviors, subsequent research has established effects on both, possibly reflecting the greater role that contemporary women play in their families' economic lives (McLoyd et al., 1994; Conger et al. 1994). There is a pressing need for continued research on familial factors that might mediate poor children's long-term adjustment. As Huston (1994a) has said, developmental psychologists are often reluctant to pursue family process models of poverty for fear of being seen as perpetuating the "culture of poverty" view (Lewis, 1966), which entails blaming the victims. However, one might argue that precisely because such views have been and continue to be put forth by many, it is incumbent on developmentalists to continue their empirical study of the challenges facing poor parents and their children. Systematic research in this area can be invaluable not only in raising general awareness of the diverse psychological adversities that confront families in poverty, but also in guiding the design of future interventions and policies which can, expediently and efficaciously, promote positive outcomes among these vulnerable groups of individuals.

Cumulative Risk and Protection Models

The likelihood of negative child outcomes is substantially increased when low socioeconomic status coexists with other family risk factors such as large family size, severe marital discord, paternal criminality, and maternal mental illness. Widely cited research by Rutter (1979) showed that such risk factors considered individually did not increase the likelihood of negative outcomes. On the other hand, the presence of two risk factors resulted in a fourfold increase in the incidence of mental disorder, and the presence of four factors was associated with a tenfold increase in risk.

Consonant results have subsequently been reported by several research teams. Sameroff, Seifer, Zax, and Barocas (1987) considered 10 variables that are correlates of economic deprivation, including parents' occupation and educational status, family size, and maternal mental health and parenting behaviors, and found that multiple co-occurring risks substantially increased preschool children's maladjustment. More recently, these investigators reported similar findings with an adolescent cohort, wherein increases in the number of risks experienced were linked with substantial declines particularly in the realms of psychological adjustment and academic performance[1] (Sameroff et al., 1997; see also Luster and McAdoo, 1994).

Based on their own data as well as others, Shaw and colleagues (1994) argued that whereas multiple familial adversities are detrimental for children in general, their ill-effects can be particularly pronounced for those living in poverty. Children in middle-class families can often be buffered against disturbances in their parents' functioning by diverse ecosystemic factors, such as access to relatively high quality support services within their schools and communities. For poor youth, by contrast, the adverse effects of intra-familial stressors are often compounded by the additional ecocultural hardships that accompany life in unremitting poverty.

Parallel to the negative effects that stem from co-occurring adversities, cumulative *beneficial* effects can derive from coexisting protective factors. Empirical evidence in this regard has been presented by two research teams (Jessor et al., 1995; Fergusson & Lynskey, 1996). Each of these teams developed composites encompassing various previously established correlates of resilience, including individual attributes of the children, as well as positive aspects of relationships with family and peers. The underlying argument was that multiple, coexisting protective factors are more likely to result in resilient functioning than one or two such factors existing in isolation. Consistent with this reasoning, findings in one case showed that while children with a single protective factor showed high vulnerability to problem behaviors in the face of adversities, those with multiple protection indices seemed relatively unaffected (Jessor et al., 1995). In the second investigation, similarly, among children with multiple protective factors (those in the top quintile), an impressive 85% were found to be resilient to developing behavior problems (Fergusson & Lynskey, 1996).

Genetic Effects

Up to this point, familial influences among disadvantaged families have generally been discussed in terms of environmental effects (e.g., of particular parental behaviors on children) with no explicit reference to genetic contributions. There is a growing body of evidence, however, that genetic factors contribute substantially not only to family environment and child outcomes, but also to the observed *association between these* (for reviews, see Plomin, 1994; 1995). For example, there is evidence that genetic factors may explain between two-thirds and three-quarters of the phenotypic association between mothers' levels of negativity and adjustment problems among their adolescent children (Plomin, 1995).

The long-standing controversy regarding genetic versus environmental effects underlying familial influences is vividly reflected in two recent articles concerning disadvantaged families. In the first of these, Rowe and Rodgers (1998) critiqued the 1994 special issue of the journal *Child Development* which was focused on children and poverty (several papers from this volume have been discussed here in the section on "Families as Mediators").

Among Rowe and Rodgers' arguments were contentions that (1) articles in the *Child Development* special issue generally overstated the environmentally mediated effects of poverty on children and neglected genetic influences, (2) genetic and environmental effects were confounded in most of these studies, thus precluding conclusions about purely "environmental" effects, and (3) behavior-genetic studies reflect the design of choice for future research on families in poverty.

Counter-arguments are seen in a companion paper by Huston, McLoyd, and Garcia Coll (1998), editors of the *Child Development* special issue. These authors noted that because children in poverty are often exposed to extreme environmental adversities, the relative influence of these forces as compared to genetic ones is likely to be greater among them as compared to affluent youth.[2] They further argued that while behavioral genetic studies do provide information about heritability, they are constrained in their potential for illuminating environmental influences. Huston and colleagues concluded their review with an exhortation for more research of an interdisciplinary nature, views shared by many behavioral geneticists (see Rende & Plomin, 1993; Kendler, 1995), which incorporates strong assessments of genetic constructs as well as sophisticated views of environmental influences.

For future research on mechanisms underlying familial risks, there is obvious value to such interdisciplinary efforts; yet for those concerned with identifying relatively "modifiable modifiers" in the lives of poor children, the intensive scrutiny of genetic mechanisms is not necessarily as critical. Behavior genetic designs that tease apart genetic versus environmental influences are clearly essential when seeking to understand the processes underlying familial effects on children. For many, however, the central focus is on ascertaining the relative significance of specific risk and protective factors. And when such researchers do demonstrate the potency of particular aspects of family functioning (e.g., child maltreatment versus other familial factors or facets of the community or the child), they can provide important directions for interventions, even if the construct in question was in fact strongly influenced by genes. Evidence that a particular characteristic is transmitted genetically by no means implies that it is immutable to change via environmental interventions: ". . . heritability does not imply untreatability" (Plomin, 1995; p. 33).

SUMMARY

1. Developmental research on disadvantaged parents' psychopathology has been focused largely on mothers with little attention to fathers. Mothers living in poverty show heightened vulnerability to depression, and their distress, in turn, can affect various aspects of their behaviors including aspects of parenting. Inner-city families are also vulnerable to substance abuse. Parental drug abuse is linked with parenting problems as well as child psychopathology, with children's adjustment problems escalating the longer they live with an addicted caregiver. Contrary to widespread stereotypes, many drug-abusing mothers are cognizant of their difficulties around parenting, and can be both receptive and responsive to sensitive intervention programs aimed at promoting their efficacy as individuals and parents.

2. Aspects of mothers' developmental histories, such as adversities encountered during their own childhoods, are often reflected in the quality of their interactions with their children. Positive maternal attributes such as emotional well-being, optimism, and high self-esteem can serve important protective effects for poor children's psychosocial adjustment. By contrast, the ramifications of high parental IQ appear to be more equivocal.

Frequent life stressors exacerbate the vulnerability of disadvantaged parents as well as their children. Furthermore, negative life events can affect poor youth more profoundly than their affluent counterparts, given radical differences in availability of various "safety nets" to shield them from adversities they encounter.

Among families in dangerous, inner-city neighborhoods, close parental supervision and firm, consistent discipline can be critical in reducing risk for various negative child outcomes, including predilections to aggressive behaviors, substance use, and disavowal of academics.

3. A warm and supportive parent-child relationship can substantially reduce risks linked with poverty at various developmental stages. On the other hand, high levels of overall family cohesion may, for some youth, represent discomfitingly high blurring of boundaries between family members.

4. Although poverty is associated with elevated risk for child maltreatment, links are attenuated when other variables, particularly aspects of parents' psychopathology, are taken into account. Studies have shown that maltreated children living in poverty reflect maladjustment in several

domains. Underlying processes that can be implicated include deficits in affective and cognitive processes and disturbances in the quality of attachments with caregivers.

Findings on the substantial role of parental distress in child maltreatment, along with those showing escalating problems among maltreated children, jointly attest to the urgent need for early prevention efforts that target disadvantaged parents who are vulnerable to high life stress and psychiatric distress.

5. Disturbances in family functioning appear to mediate some of the ill-effects of poverty on children. However, large portions of unexplained variability in child outcomes indicate the potential importance of additional paths of influence. These include extra-familial or community-level forces, as well as nonpsychopathological aspects of parents' functioning such as their positive psychological attributes, and their success at meeting the most fundamental needs of their families including those for food, shelter, and health care.

6. Multiple coexisting risks substantially increase the vulnerability of children in poverty. Conversely, multiple co-occurring protective factors are more likely than are single ones, to be linked with resilient functioning among children experiencing adversities.

7. Associations between familial factors and child outcomes may derive from genetic links as well as environmentally-mediated influences. Even in instances where genetic factors largely underlie links between parental maladjustment and child psychopathology, however, this does not imply that the problems in either generation are immutable to change. Heritability of behavioral or emotional dimensions does not denote imperviousness to prevention or treatment interventions.

NOTES

1. Similar findings have been obtained in the New Zealand Christchurch Study (Fergusson, Horwood, & Lynskey, 1994). Considering multiple childhood adversities including social, economic, child-rearing, and family risks, children in the most disadvantaged 5% of the cohort had risks of developing multiple problems as teenagers that were over 100 times greater than risks faced by the 50% of the cohort in the most advantaged group. Further, an index based on a linear combination of multiple risks was a far stronger predictor of childhood outcomes than were single demographic indices related to SES or family living standards (Fergusson & Lynskey, 1996).

2. Support for this suggestion is evident in writings by behavioral-geneticists as well. For example, Plomin (1995) has cautioned that existing findings of strong genetic influences in links between family environment and child outcomes are based largely on work with middle-class families and may not generalize to extremes of family environments. Similarly, studies have shown that even among middle-class families, the relative strength of genetic influences varies depending on the parental behavior considered. To illustrate, there are strong genetic influences for parental *warmth* (positive parental responses are elicited by positive child dispositions; see Plomin, 1994; 1995) but not parental *control,* which is less likely to be determined by children's dispositions than by other factors. By the same token, one might argue that impoverished parents' behaviors are more likely to be multiply determined than those of others; the vicissitudes of their everyday lives could profoundly affect their "genetically dictated" parenting dispositions.

5

EXOSYSTEMIC INFLUENCES

Mr. Cabrera landed in Pasadena at the age of 10, short and skinny and intimidated. By 13, quick on his feet and agile with his fists, he had dropped out of middle school to devote himself to fighting.

His mother was very upset, but he told her it was the only way to survive in their neighborhood. The choice was not whether to join a gang but which one, he said.

He elected Mara Salvatrucha, a gang formed by Salvadoran immigrants in Los Angeles that is now pan-Hispanic. . . . After his initiation, which was a severe beating, he had MS tattooed on his chest.

"MS totally gave me a feel of belonging," he said, demonstrating the hand signs that serve as the gang greeting.

By 16, he was chief of the gang's Hollywood chapter. Between the ages of 18 and 22, he accumulated 14 aliases and a rap sheet that included two dozen arrests and six felony convictions. . . .

"We knew we were doing bad things, but bad things were valued as good things in our world," he said. "We were confused."

—Sontag, 1997; *New York Times,* August 11, p. A8

For many poor children, informal support systems within their communities can play a critical role in helping them cope with ongoing stressors of life in poverty. By the same token, families living in urban ghettos—the locus of some of the most concentrated and extreme forms of poverty in contemporary America—must contend with a constant barrage of neighborhood-level forces that are pernicious for the social and psychological adjustment of their developing children.

In this chapter, community influences that affect families in poverty are discussed in four sections. These are focused, respectively, on the effects of informal support networks involving extended family and community members; the quality of the physical environment with special attention to homelessness; characteristics of neighborhoods in terms of sociodemographic composition and cohesiveness among neighbors; and effects of community violence across the developmental spectrum.

SUPPORT NETWORKS

Support From Extended Kin

Several studies involving African American families have shown that extended kin support is a common response to harsh economic conditions and can promote positive outcomes among both parents and children (Apfel & Seitz, 1997; Stevens, 1988; Wilson, 1984). The benefits of social supports for parents' functioning are evident not only in increases in positive outcomes such as greater psychological well-being and positive parenting behaviors, but also reductions in negative parenting practices (Belsky, 1980; Burchinal et al., 1996; Taylor, Casten, & Flickinger, 1993). For example, inner-city mothers with high levels of perceived support tend to display relatively few depressive symptoms, experience less negativity about the parental role, and use less punishment (McLoyd et al., 1994). By the same token, feelings of social isolation and loneliness characterize low-SES parents who are neglectful of their children more so than those who are not (Gaudin, Polansky, Kilpatrick, & Shilton, 1993).

Perceptions of social support may be more critical for disadvantaged individuals than support actually used (Berman et al., 1996). There is evidence that actual receipt of help from others (e.g., with child care) is linked with lower levels of problematic child-rearing behavior among low-income parents and their more affluent counterparts alike (Hashima & Amato, 1994). By contrast, expectations of adequate social support in crisis situations appear to be advantageous for low-income families more so than others. Given the paucity of their resources and the multiplicity of their life stressors, convictions that help will be forthcoming when needed may be particularly comforting to parents who contend with conditions of serious economic disadvantage (Hashima & Amato, 1994).

Apfel and Seitz's (1996) work with low-income mothers in multigenerational households suggests curvilinear associations between teenage mothers' well-being and the level of support received from their own mothers.

Arrangements most likely to result in eventual self-sufficiency were those in which grandmothers provided help with child-rearing tasks in moderation, rather than either replacing the mother as the primary caregiver, or providing only minimal help. Findings such as these attest to the value of providing teen mothers with both psychological support, and tangible help with child-rearing, to a moderate degree. Such forms of assistance can help many young mothers in poverty to maximally develop their own capacities for independence and effective parenting over the long term.

For disadvantaged children, the beneficial effects of extended kin support can occur directly or indirectly, via their parents' adjustment (see McLoyd & Wilson, 1990, 1991). Grandparents often provide substantial emotional and material support directly to their grandchildren; in fact, they may sometimes be more willing to offer support to grandchildren than their own children, particularly when the latter have problems of substance abuse (Apfel & Seitz, 1997). Indirect effects involving parents are evident in findings that kin support can bolster parents' authoritative parenting behaviors, feelings of well-being, and involvement in children's schools, benefits which are reflected, in turn, across several domains of child adaptation including behavioral conformity and school achievement (Taylor, 1996; Taylor et al., 1993).

Involvement in Religion

Involvement in religion and church membership can also serve important protective functions for poor parents' child-rearing behaviors and for positive outcomes among their children (Baldwin et al., 1990; Brody, Stoneman, & Flor, 1996; Kelley et al., 1992; Werner & Smith, 1992). Religious beliefs can facilitate positive adjustment by providing a support network of others in the church community, by enhancing positive beliefs of the self, and by leading to the use of prayer rather than maladaptive coping strategies (e.g., alcohol consumption) for negotiating life crises and everyday stressors (Brody et al., 1996; Garcia Coll & Vasquez Garcia, 1995; Masten et al., 1990).

Strong beliefs in the supernatural may, however, become counterproductive if they take the form of fatalism. Although embedded in religion, fatalism or beliefs that cultural patterns and hierarchies are predetermined, can result in convictions that nothing can be done to improve one's life circumstances. In interaction with the overt oppression and discrimination that many poor minority families face, such fatalistic belief systems can create formidable barriers to improving the overall quality of disadvantaged families' life situations (Garcia Coll & Vasquez Garcia, 1995).

School Experiences

Although American children generally show deteriorating interest in academics across the school years (Lepper, Sethi, Dialdin, & Drake, 1997), this problem is typically exacerbated for children in poverty. Noting the accelerated risks for academic failure typically observed among poor youth over time, Stipek (1997) has emphasized influences not only in the home and neighborhood (e.g., low family support for school work or high exposure to traumatic life events), but also characteristics of many schools serving disadvantaged youth. Teachers in these settings, for example, often have low academic expectations of their students, prophecies which are all-too-often self-fulfilling. In addition, many use strategies which (though well-meaning) can further undermine their students' self-confidence and motivation to learn, such as indiscriminate praise, or sympathy for failure at academic tasks (Comer, 1988). Even the most able and committed of teachers face several obstacles in educating their students. Apart from being poorly paid, most receive scant training or supervision for working with children's adjustment disturbances, which many of their students are vulnerable to as a result of ongoing exposure to poverty and community violence. "Many teachers experience the same feelings of frustration, failure, and hopelessness that their students feel. . . .Unless teachers are given the support they need to succeed, many children will continue to fail." (Stipek, 1997, pp. 88-89).

Those children who do have positive experiences at school can be at a substantial advantage over others (Felner et al., 1985; Posner & Vandell, 1994; Rutter, 1990; Werner & Smith, 1992), and once again, positive school experiences may often yield greater benefits to disadvantaged youth as compared to their affluent counterparts. Dubois and colleagues (1992; 1994), for example, demonstrated that the salutary effects of support from school staff were stronger among poor youth than others. Based on their findings, these researchers suggested that for children facing multiple risks, the relative paucity of positive experiences outside school may render all the more salient, those that occur within school.

Benefits of positive experiences at school are also reflected in data on students' placement in gifted classrooms. Among low-income African American elementary school students, those placed in gifted classrooms have been found to fare better than potentially gifted children placed in nongifted classrooms (Ford & Harris, 1996). Advantages were apparent across a range of indices encompassing their own achievement ideology, perceived parental achievement orientation, and attitudes toward high achievers at school. Differences such as these may reflect various advantages of placement in self-contained gifted programs, including exposure to relatively challenging curricula, relative protection from peer pressure against negative achievement, as well as beneficial effects on children's self-esteem, of being labeled as gifted (Ford & Harris, 1996).

In a parallel vein, however, placement of children in low-track programs can exacerbate preexisting differences among students in both self-perception and competence. Disadvantaged students placed in lower level tracks rarely move into higher ones for several reasons, including exposure to instruction that is of inferior quality, and which emphasizes basic skills rather than higher-order learning. Furthermore, low-track students are often aware of reduced long-term life opportunities given their restricted curriculum, and as a result, progressively lose interest in academics (National Research Council, 1993). For disadvantaged students in general, therefore, any potential gains of ability tracking for the more intellectually gifted youth must be carefully weighed against the discouragement that can derive for their less intelligent peers, a group already at heightened risk for both scholastic and behavior problems (Chapter 2).

Peer Relations

Whereas support from peers can contribute to positive outcomes among at-risk children (Cauce, 1986; Werner & Smith, 1992), studies have revealed increasingly complex associations between peer acceptance and children's behavioral adjustment. Among Black boys from lower- and lower-middle income families, some forms of aggression, such as reactive aggression and bullying (in the service of establishing dominance with peers) appear to be acceptable or even approved of, by their first grade peers (Coie, Dodge, Terry, & Wright, 1991; Dodge, Coie, Pettit, & Price, 1990). Popular first graders tend to engage in more bullying than average first graders. By the third grade level, by contrast, such aggressive behaviors appear to be poorly tolerated by peers. Commenting on these differences, authors of these studies suggest that at the time of entry into school, behaviors that reflect standing up for oneself may represent a useful strategy for establishing one's social position. By the third grade level, on the other hand, children have typically developed more sophisticated evaluation schemes which allow them to distinguish between bullying and leadership, and justified versus unjustified forms of reactive aggression.

During the later childhood years, nonconforming behavior patterns among disadvantaged youth are often associated with overall positive status in the peer group. Whereas it is well-known that deviant youth tend to form personal friendships with others also deviant (e.g., Coie, Terry, Zakriski, & Lochman, 1995; Dishion, Andrews, & Crosby, 1995), recent research has shown, further, that even the wider peer group may endorse anti-establishment behaviors. Among highly stressed, disadvantaged fourth, fifth, and sixth graders who displayed high levels of antisocial behaviors, many reported that their peers offered them high social support (Dubow, Edwards, & Ippolito, 1997). Eighth grade students who associate with deviant peers have been found to be generally well accepted by the peer group as a whole (Coie et al., 1995). Similarly, positive peer status among inner-city high school students can sometimes be linked with prosocial, responsible behavior patterns. Equally often, however, it coexists with high levels of aggressive-disruptive and nonconforming behaviors in the school setting (Luthar & McMahon, 1996; Seidman et al., 1994).

Parallel disconcerting trends involving positive peer status are evident in relation to other adjustment indices, including substance use and academic performance. Significant links have been identified between preteen children's peer competence and their levels of substance use (Wills, Vaccaro, & McNamara, 1992). High achieving inner-city youth often struggle with the conflict between achieving the approval of peers on the one hand, and excelling academically, on the other (Arroyo & Zigler, 1995); as indicated previously, disadvantaged adolescents who enjoy high status in their peer group can show deteriorating grades over time (Luthar, 1995).

Such interdomain links involving peer status might derive largely from potent sociocultural forces. The apparent endorsement of aggression by the peer group, for example, may reflect the subculture of violence that is often embedded in the context of poverty and restricted life opportunities (Hammond & Yung, 1993). In inner-city communities besieged by crime, aggressive behaviors can be linked with relatively high prestige (Coie & Jacobs, 1993; Luthar, 1997; Richters & Cicchetti, 1993). Behaviors which most adults would term as "deviant" are often the very behaviors that help adolescents in these communities maintain a sense of high self-esteem and a feeling of belonging to a valued peer group.

Similar explanations might be offered for the peer group's ostensible antipathy toward academic success. As argued for minority children in particular (Chapter 3), poor children in general are often unconvinced that success at school can lead to success in later life. Many of these youth are (often unsurprisingly) disenchanted with all that academics represents, a disillusionment which can result in substantial peer pressure away from academic effort (Cauce, 1986; Luthar, 1997).

Two questions warranting further attention derive from this body of work on peer status and behavioral nonconformity, the first of which is whether the trends described reflect an adolescent phenomenon more so than an inner city phenomenon (Luthar, 1997). As Moffitt (1993a) has argued, during the developmental moratorium of adolescence in contemporary Western society, antisocial behaviors can take on a positive value because they symbolize maturity and independence. In a similar vein are Steinberg's (1987) suggestions that U.S. teenagers in general, regardless of their sociocultural background, do not particularly admire hard work at school, views that have garnered support in empirical research (e.g., Wentzel & Asher, 1995). What remains to be determined is the degree to which such "adolescent traits" may have particularly pronounced long-term ramifications for youth in poverty. These youngsters face many more adversities than their affluent counterparts, and concomitantly are less exposed to resolute support for (and pressure toward) school success from adults in their homes, schools, and wider communities (Luthar & Burack, in press).

The second question involves a fine-grained appraisal of the type of nonconformity that peers appreciate: precisely which forms and degrees of aggressive and disruptive behaviors are admired by peers and which are disdained? Coie and colleagues (1995) suggest that whereas aggressiveness in itself may not adversely affect peer status, it is poorly tolerated if it coexists with social insensitivity, lack of empathy, and self-regulation failures (Coie, Terry, Lenox, Lochman, & Hyman, 1995). Similarly, Moffitt's (1993) thesis raises the question of whether inner-city adolescents, or all adolescents, are as tolerant of flagrant delinquency as they appear to be of some disruptive or aggressive behaviors. Notwithstanding an admiration of peers with the mettle to buck the system, it is more than likely that inner-city teens in general, like affluent youth, would draw the line at actively extolling acts of egregious victimization of others or serious violations of the law.

THE PHYSICAL ENVIRONMENT

Poverty in Rural Versus Urban Areas

Recent research on adaptation among disadvantaged children has been overwhelmingly focused on the urban poor, possibly as a result of the conspicuous and burgeoning problems of inner-city ghettos, as well as their physical proximity to major research universities (Huston et al., 1994). Yet, childhood poverty is as prevalent, if not more so, in rural America, and there is a need for far more empirical research on risk and protective processes that affect poor children in these areas. Findings obtained with their urban counterparts cannot simply be assumed to generalize to rural children (Rutter, 1989b), for there are substantial differences in experiences of rural versus urban poverty in terms of spatial characteristics of communities, characteristics of support systems, as well as family structure. To illustrate, the environment in urban ghettos is characterized by high adult unemployment, rampant racism, ever-present threats of violence, and often, a high proportion of single-parent households. Poor rural parents, on the other hand, receive fewer welfare benefits and lower wages for work than their urban counterparts (Huston, 1994a). They also have less access to emotionally supportive, cohesive networks, and can be more prone to using coercive, punitive practices in child rearing, possibly as a result of low emotional support and/or salient ideological beliefs (e.g., emphasis on compliance in agrarian communities) (MacPhee Fritz, & Miller-Heyl, 1996). Differences such as these attest to the pressing need for greater attention to the salient processes that can shape the personal and social adjustment of poor children in rural areas.

Quality of Physical Environment

Demoralizing housing conditions frequently exacerbate what McLoyd and Wilson (1994) have called the "strain of living poor." Residents in public housing projects routinely contend with conditions detrimental not only to their physical health, but also to their sense of dignity; including overcrowding, peeling lead-based paint, infestation by insects and rodents, and inadequate plumbing, conditions that must also inevitably affect their capacity as caregivers (e.g., Giovannoni & Billingsley, 1970).

The effects of adverse physical environments is perhaps most poignantly reflected in research on homeless mothers. These parents are frequently exposed to high noise levels, crowdedness, physically hazardous living conditions, and a chronic lack of privacy, problems which compound the strains of trying to meet basic needs of food, income, health, and long-term housing for their children (Boxill & Beaty, 1990; Hausman & Hammen, 1993; Koblinsky, Morgan, & Anderson, 1997). As might be expected, exposure to such adversities is related to high rates of psychiatric distress. In a homeless shelter in Los Angeles County, Zima, Wells, Benjamin, & Duan (1996) found that almost three in every four mothers indicated symptoms of a lifetime major mental disorder and/or high current psychological distress.

The challenges of "public mothering" also affect parenting behaviors. Establishing and maintaining order and family routines is often difficult for homeless mothers due to the lack of privacy and the frequently arbitrary

nature of shelter rules (Boxill & Beaty, 1990). Among the mothers themselves, conflicts often arise about misbehavior of their children, which in turn
adversely affects parent-child relationships as well as the self-esteem of both
mothers and their children (Boxill & Beaty, 1990; Hausman & Hammen,
1993).

As compared to their low-income housed counterparts, homeless mothers
manifest more problems across both parenting and psychiatric domains. They
tend to display less warmth and affection toward their children, as well as
less variety in social and cultural experiences and academic stimulation
(Koblinsky et al., 1997). Rates of drug abuse can be up to three times higher
among homeless mothers as compared to poor housed women, and problems
of alcohol abuse up to five times as high (Zima et al., 1996). Furthermore,
the high mental health needs of these homeless mothers typically remain
largely unmet: surveys have shown that less than one in five receive services
for their psychiatric difficulties (Zima et al., 1996).

As with their parents, homelessness is linked with heightened vulnerability
among poor children as well. A study involving preschoolers living in shelters
showed that as compared to their housed peers, these youngsters had poorer
self-concepts and saw themselves as being less well accepted by their
mothers (DiBiase & Waddell, 1995). In addition, teachers gave them lower
ratings on cognitive competence, and higher ratings on depression, social
withdrawal, and schizoid behavior. Similarly, among 6- to 11-year-old African American children in a homeless shelter, teacher reports indicated
significant problems across multiple symptom domains, as well as significant
deficits in everyday adaptive behaviors (Masten et al., 1997).

In sum, homeless children constitute a particularly vulnerable subgroup of
disadvantaged youth. These youngsters often contend with inordinately high
levels of parental psychological distress and scant access to mental health
services, pressures inevitably compounded by life in temporary shelters
where resources are stretched thin and daily schedules unpredictable at best,
and tumultuous at worst.

NEIGHBORHOODS

During the last two decades, there has been a resurgence of research interest
in the effects of the neighborhood on children's functioning. In the early part
of the 20th century, neighborhood and community influences were often
prominently featured in scientific discussions of salient influences in the lives
of American families (Ensminger et al., 1996). Interest in these issues waned

during the 1970s and 1980s, as sociologists focused more on family affili-
ation and social stratification in explaining educational and occupational
attainment. The recent renewed interest in the neighborhood may reflect
growing recognition among scientists that (1) the primary social contexts for
many young people in contemporary society are located in their neighborhoods, given their restricted mobility within cities; and (2) the effects of
neighborhoods may be particularly pronounced in inner-city settings, due to
increasing isolation among families in impoverished areas (Ensminger et al.,
1996). In discussions that follow, salient research findings regarding neighborhoods effects on poor children and families are summarized.

Characteristics of Neighborhood: Effects on Children

Preschool children growing up in neighborhoods with a high proportion
of low-income families reflect heightened vulnerability to externalizing
problems such as aggressive behaviors (Duncan et al., 1994). Conversely,
among low-income, elementary school-age children, living in a middle-SES
neighborhood can serve significant protective functions in terms of children's
levels of aggression (Kupersmidt, Griesler, DeRosier, Patterson, & Davis,
1995). Consonant trends have been documented among preadolescents and
adolescents (Attar et al., 1994; see also Chapter 2). In a study involving
African American seventh and eighth graders from diverse socioeconomic
backgrounds, significant links were reported between family members' perceptions of neighborhood risk levels, and reports of externalizing, undercon-
trolled behavior problems among children (Mason et al., 1994). Associations
have also been documented between inner-city junior high students' perceptions of danger in their neighborhoods and their own levels of alcohol and
marijuana use (Dembo, Blount, Schmeidler, & Burgos, 1986).

The influence of neighborhoods may also vary according to the economic
climate of the broader geographical region within which they are located.
Analyses of data from the National Longitudinal Survey for Youth (Chase-
Lansdale & Gordon, 1996) indicated that overall effects of neighborhood on
child outcomes, considered at the national level, were modest. However,
associations were considerably stronger in some parts of the country—that
is, the Northeast and Midwestern regions—as compared to others (the South
and West). Discussing these findings, the authors argued that during the
1980s, which was when families in this study were assessed, the Northeast
and Midwestern regions of the U.S. experienced severe economic decline
whereas the Southern and Western areas witnessed a surge in various employment sectors. For children in the former regions, therefore, positive

neighborhood factors such as high SES and racial similarity of neighbors may have served substantial protective influences against adversities linked with increasing poverty during the 1980s.

Various mechanisms via which neighborhoods might affect children have been summarized by Brooks-Gunn (1995), in a paper integrating the views of several influential writers including W. J. Wilson (1987, 1991). Effects can occur via *collective socialization*, or the influence of norms, sanctions, and reciprocity among neighbors; the availability of *neighborhood resources*, such as libraries, community centers, and high-quality child care; *contagion*, e.g., the greater risk for behaviors such as out-of-wedlock pregnancies when they are common in the community; and *social disorganization*, which encompasses each of the previously mentioned mechanisms.

Neighborhood Effects on Maltreatment and Violence

A dearth of informal resources and support systems in their neighborhoods can be implicated in heightened risk for child maltreatment among disadvantaged parents (Eckenrode et al., 1995). Garbarino and his colleagues (see Garbarino & Sherman, 1980) identified some neighborhoods which had higher rates of child maltreatment than would be expected based on socioeconomic conditions alone. They found that parents in these neighborhoods rarely made constructive use of informal supports (such as youth groups), generally relied on formal public agencies when interventions were necessary, and more often tried to exploit others during exchanges. Conversely, parents in neighborhoods with lower than expected maltreatment rates experienced greater satisfaction with their neighborhoods as contexts for family and child development, and also made active attempts to shield their children from the dangers of their environments.

Structural features of communities can also be related to variations in risk for child maltreatment. Rates of officially reported maltreatment have been found to be particularly high in areas with the interrelated conditions of poverty, unemployment, female-headed households, racial segregation, abandoned housing, and population loss (Coulton, Korbin, Su, & Chow, 1995). Processes possibly underlying these findings include, again, feelings of distrust and limited interaction among neighbors, reluctance to intervene when witnessing unruly behaviors among children, and tendencies among families who can afford it, to leave the "undesirable" neighborhood, thus taking with them skills, resources, and prosocial influences (Coulton et al., 1995).

Collective efficacy, or high cohesion among neighbors and willingness to intervene for the common good, can be critical not only for reduced levels of violence within families, but also at a broader level within neighborhoods and communities. In research involving almost 350 neighborhoods in Chicago, collective efficacy was inversely linked with multiple measures of violence, and also partially mediated or explained links between concentrated disadvantage and indices of violence in the community (Sampson, Raudenbush, & Earls, 1997). In sum, there is considerable evidence that fostering a shared sense of community responsibility among neighbors in inner-city areas can contribute greatly to reduced levels of violence, both among family members and within communities.

VIOLENCE IN THE NEIGHBORHOOD

Youngsters living in inner-city areas are exposed to alarmingly high rates of violence as both witnesses and victims. Consider the following statistics.

- In a low-income, moderately violent area in Washington, D.C., almost 9 of 10 first and second graders surveyed reported they had witnessed at least one arrest, and over one-third said they had witnessed a dead body outside on at least one occasion (Richters & Martinez, 1993).
- In a study of 6th, 8th, and 10th graders in New Haven, CT, 40% reported witnessing at least one shooting or stabbing in the previous year; almost three out of four reported feeling unsafe in one or more environmental contexts (Schwab-Stone et al., 1995).
- Among inner-city high-school students in the greater Miami area, 87% had witnessed a mugging or beating, and 38% were actually victims of such events. Almost 42% of the students had witnessed a murder (Berman et al., 1996).

Effects on Children's Adjustment

The trauma that results from children's exposure to community violence, especially pronounced when they are personally victimized (Fitzpatrick, 1993), is manifested in varying ways across the developmental spectrum (Garbarino, 1995; Osofsky, 1995). Infants and toddlers may present with increased irritability and sleep disturbances, fears of being alone, and regression in developmental achievements such as toileting and language; the development of secure attachments to adults can also be threatened (Marans & Adelman, 1997). Among preschool and school-age children, common signs include disturbances in sleep and concentration, as well as increases in anxiety and depression (Marans & Adelman, 1997; Martinez & Richters, 1993). Older children exposed to community violence commonly display depressive problems as well as symptoms of posttraumatic stress disorder (DuRant et al., 1995; Garbarino, 1995; Singer, Anglin, Song, & Lunghofer, 1995). Freeman and colleagues (1993) reported that among 6- to 12-year old children who were exposed to at least one traumatic event directed at themselves, a relative, or a friend, almost 40% exhibited levels of depression warranting clinical concern. In other research involving inner-city adolescents, almost 35% of those exposed to at least one violent event met full criteria for psychiatric diagnoses of posttraumatic stress disorder (Berman et al., 1996).

Apart from intrapsychic distress, violence exposure can also heighten children's own predilections toward aggression, with effects documented as early as the preschool years. Garbarino, Kostelny, and Dubrow (1991) provide reports of preschoolers ". . . playing at shooting-up drugs, strutting like 'gang-bangers', and taking turns being victims, mourners, and preachers as they acted out the common occurrence of funerals resulting from gang warfare" (p. 139). Research involving elementary school students and adolescents has shown that while violence exposure is linked with various problems including depression, substance use, and academic problems, among the strongest associations are those with aggressive, antisocial behaviors (Schwab-Stone et al., 1995).

A medley of psychological and ecocultural forces can converge in increasing overall risk for externalizing problems among youth exposed to neighborhood violence. These include the tendencies of young children to identify with aggressive adults in their communities, the implicit promise of gang membership to provide youth with physical protection and camaraderie as well as prestige and power in the local community, and the allure of crime for children growing up in conditions of abject poverty (Coie & Jacobs, 1993; Garbarino, 1995; National Research Council, 1993; Richters & Cicchetti, 1993). The social disorganization of violent communities, their psychological and physical isolation from mainstream society, and the dearth of available opportunities for youth to achieve goals in socially approved ways, conjointly further erode young people's bonds to conventional society and foster, instead, bonding with antisocial peers (Elliott, Huizinga, & Ageton, 1985; Hawkins & Weis, 1985).

Effects of community violence on children's adaptation may also be partially mediated via changes in parents' attitudes and behaviors. Some parents in dangerous neighborhoods, for example, may become relatively tolerant of their children's aggressive behaviors, feeling that children may need to defend themselves from others (Dodge et al., 1994). On the other hand, many become overprotective or even controlling. For many families in chronically violent communities, children's increasing independence and normal exploration can jeopardize their safety and are thus sharply curtailed (Osofsky, 1995).

Protective parenting strategies can yield substantial benefits for children's adaptive behaviors. Richters and Martinez (1993) found that among inner-city youth living in homes rated as stable (by school teachers) and safe (as per child reports of seeing guns/drugs at home), less than 1 in 10 showed significant behavior problems, as judged by teacher- and parent-reports. The odds for adaptational failures increased by 300% for children in homes rated as either unstable or unsafe, and by more than 1,500% for children in homes viewed as both unstable and unsafe. As noted at several points previously (Chapters 3 and 4), these findings once again suggest benefits when parents are able to maintain high levels of stability and safety within the "proximal" socializing environment of the home.

Lest such an encouraging message be overinterpreted, it is critical to emphasize that for inner-city parents to maintain stable and resource-rich home environments—while themselves contending with relentless poverty and community turbulence, along with, frequently, serious psychiatric problems and social isolation—presents no small challenge. While applauding the strengths of those parents who seem to shield their young from community adversities with some success, it is important to remain cognizant of the substantial obstacles that all families who live in chronically violent and disenfranchised communities must overcome, in order to achieve such outcomes in any sustained way.

SUMMARY

1. Support from extended kin can serve substantial protective effects for families in poverty. The salutary effects of kin support on children can operate both directly (e.g., from grandparents to grandchildren) and indirectly, via the mediating route of parents' adjustment.

2. For poor families, religious beliefs and church membership can be beneficial, ostensibly due to the expansion of informal support networks as well as the use of relatively adaptive coping strategies. However, beliefs in the supernatural can also take the counterproductive guise of fatalistic beliefs that life circumstances are unchangeable.

3. Positive school experiences, including support from teachers and exposure to optimally challenging curricula, can serve important protective effects for children in poverty. Conversely, experiences that attenuate academic motivation, such as low teacher expectations and placement in low-track programs, can increase risks for school failure. In many schools serving underprivileged youth, not only the students themselves but also their teachers are often in great need of additional support, e.g., in the form of ongoing training and supervision in innovative, effective strategies for teaching, as well as for managing children's behavior problems in the classroom.

4. Whereas support from peers is often beneficial, peer popularity among disadvantaged youth has shown links with not only with prosocial profiles, but also with aggressive, disruptive behaviors and poor academic performance. Explanations include the possibility that (1) peers may sometimes respect aggressiveness as reflecting self-protective, assertive behavior; (2) the associations reflect sociocultural forces within inner-cities, such as rampant community violence and disillusionment in the value of academics for future success; and (3) to some degree, trends such as these may characterize contemporary adolescents in general, rather than being unique to those in inner-city areas.

5. The adverse effects of physical environments are poignantly reflected in research on mothers and children in homeless shelters, individuals who display greater psychiatric vulnerability than their poor housed counterparts and yet receive grossly inadequate mental health care.

6. Living in disorganized, resource-poor neighborhoods can exacerbate children's risks for externalizing behaviors, as well as parents' risks for child maltreatment. Conversely, levels of violence in both homes and communities tend to be reduced when families in urban, poor neighborhoods develop high levels of cohesiveness and feelings of shared community responsibility.

7. Children who grow up in dangerous, chronically violent communities show vulnerability to multiple forms of psychiatric distress including disturbances in sleep and concentration, clinically significant levels of anxiety and depression, as well as, inevitably, heightened propensity to delinquency and violence themselves.

6

FUTURE DIRECTIONS

I nodded off a couple of times, but when my chin fell onto my chest, I was jerked awake. A woman whose baby was coughing something awful—Mama said it was the croup—asked the receptionist how much longer before she got to see someone, she need to get her baby back to bed.

The receptionist smartly flipped a page of the magazine she was reading and said, "Look, I've told you twice, they'll get to you when they can. If you didn't have time to wait, you shouldn't have come today."

The woman, sounding as if she'd just been slapped so hard she could barely speak, murmured, "I'm sorry. Thank you ma'am." Then she sat down, clutched the baby to her chest, and rocked.

I squirmed in my seat and began to think things over. Maybe the rules for how to treat poor people were written in a government manual. It probably went something like: Poor people stink. They ain't worth nothing. So treat them like they're shit on the bottom of your shoes. Stare at them coldly. Huff. Act as if their questions are stupid, even insane. When you hand them their official numbers, make sure your skin don't come in contact with theirs because God only knows where they've been and what they do behind the walls of their tar-paper shacks and tin-can trailers.

Having appraised what existing research has revealed about diverse risk and protective factors affecting disadvantaged children, we turn to directions for future work in the area. Resonant with the tenor of the book as a whole, this chapter is focused largely on directions for future scientific enquiry, with the goal of distilling broad, overarching considerations for both theoretical and research efforts concerning poor children's adjustment. Specific research questions regarding particular risk and protective processes, which have been delineated in preceding chapters, are not reiterated here.

Following directions for future enquiry is a discussion on salient thematic priorities for intervention programs, with directions derived, again, from themes which prominently emerged through the evidence reviewed in preceding chapters. Space restrictions preclude an in-depth review on procedural aspects of interventions (i.e., how major domains targeted can be effectively modified); interested readers are referred to a number of recent publications which describe promising interventions for poor children and families, involving diverse domains of adaptation (Conduct Problems Prevention Research Group, 1992; Cowen et al., 1996; Huston, 1994a; Knitzer, in press; Marans et al., 1995; McLoyd, 1997; Yoshikawa & Knitzer, 1996; Seitz, in press; Zigler, Kagan, & Hall, 1996).

The chapter concludes with a brief appraisal of pedagogical and training issues. In this section, some thoughts are presented on ways in which future scholars and practitioners might be optimally prepared for their work with children growing up in conditions of poverty.

CHILDHOOD IN POVERTY: DIRECTIONS FOR FUTURE INQUIRY

Refining Theoretical Models

There is a pressing need for more theoretical efforts on normative child development in the context of poverty, for the value of any future research on risk and protective processes must remain constrained by the degree to which it can be guided by sound conceptual models on what constitutes "normal development." Child development research to date has too often remained rooted in middle class oriented principles, with labels of deviance leveled at profiles that vary from mainstream norms (Garcia Coll et al., 1996; Luthar, 1997; Spencer et al., 1993).

Calls for theory refinement do not necessarily imply the need for entirely new theories regarding poor children; existing models can have much heuristic value if they are elaborated to specifically address themes that are salient in the lives of these youth. As Garcia Coll and colleagues (1996) have noted, the interplay between ecological (Bronfenbrenner, 1986), transactional (Sameroff & Chandler, 1975), and organizational theoretical perspectives (Sroufe & Rutter, 1984; Cicchetti & Toth, 1995) can contribute greatly to the study of risk and protective forces affecting poor children. There is, however, a need to expand such theories by explicitly incorporating major contextual themes that are powerful and unique in the lives of disadvantaged children, including forces such as societal classism and residential segregation (Garcia Coll et al., 1996; Luthar, 1997).

Such theory extension efforts are well exemplified in an integrative model for studying minority youth, presented by Garcia Coll and colleagues (1996). Anchored within social stratification theory, this model posits that there are eight major constructs that affect the development of minority children: (1) social position variables (e.g., race, social class, gender), (2) racism and discrimination, (3) segregation (residential, economic, social, and psychological), (4) promoting/inhibiting environments (school, neighborhoods, and health care), (5) adaptive culture (traditions and legacies), (6) child characteristics such as age, temperament, and physical characteristics, (7) family values and beliefs, and (8) developmental competencies including cognition, social-emotional development, and biculturalism. The attractiveness of this model lies both in the centrality accorded to several constructs that are salient in the lives of minority youth (e.g., social position, racism, and segregation) as well as in the clear specification of paths of influence, which yield, in turn, theoretical hypotheses amenable to testing in research.

It should also be noted that calls for theory refinement are not restricted to relatively overarching conceptual models (such as that of Garcia Coll and colleagues); there is value, as well, in theories of the middle range (Merton, 1968) which apply to limited ranges of data. Such theories might pertain to particular domains of adjustment, as exemplified by the writings of Elder, McLoyd, and others (Chapter 4) on familial factors as mediators of links between poverty and child adjustment. Alternatively, the focus may be on specific subgroups of children such as those of a particular ethnicity. Notwithstanding the many forces that affect poor children in general, there are obvious limits to "one-model-fits-all" approaches (Garcia Coll et al., 1996; Slaughter-Defoe, Nakagawa, Takanishi, & Johnson, 1990). Mid-range models might also pertain to particular developmental phases, focusing, for example, on the challenges of negotiating particular stage-salient tasks during early childhood, middle childhood, or adolescence among children in poverty (e.g., Luthar, 1997; Spencer & Markstron-Adamis, 1990).

Research on Normative Development

Ongoing theory refinement, in turn, presupposes the availability of pertinent data, and many have emphasized the need for more research on normative developmental processes among disadvantaged youth (Fantuzzo et al., 1996; Graham, 1992; Luthar, 1997; Zaslow & Takanishi,

1993). Again, there might be little reason to expect unique developmental processes for many facets of poor children's social-emotional adjustment. As research by Graham and her colleagues demonstrated, for example, central principles regarding social information processing, which originated in mainstream psychology, are entirely applicable when working with disadvantaged, African American youth (Graham & Hoehn, 1995; Graham & Hudley, 1994).

This having been said, it should be noted that unqualified generalizations are ill-advised when aspects of children's development are vulnerable to forces which are essentially unique to one of the cultural settings under consideration. To illustrate, inner-city children, more than their more affluent peers, contend with a marked dissonance between salient beliefs espoused by their peers and families, versus those in mainstream society. As established in previous chapters, this dissonance between microcosmic and macrocosmic belief systems can color many aspects of children's development including their academic trajectories, their peer associations, and their aspirations and goals for the future, as well as the nature of interrelations across these domains. In short, influences that are largely specific to the ecocultural context of poverty can clearly result in varying patterns of "normative" social-emotional development.

Issues of generalizability are also tied to the developmental period under consideration. As children progress along the developmental trajectory and are exposed to an ever-widening range of influences outside the home, cultural forces can assume increasing prominence in shaping the meanings and ontogenesis of different behaviors. In studying patterns of personal and social adjustment, therefore, the likelihood of observing distinctive developmental trends across subcultures is greater among preadolescent and adolescent youth as compared to toddlers or infants. In point of fact, ethnographers have established that by late childhood, even classic conceptions of development can have little validity in the context of urban ghettos (Burton et al., 1995). Inner-city African American youth do not experience adolescence as a transition period (between childhood and adulthood) due to several factors, including relatively narrow age gaps between family members, blurred intergenerational boundaries, and tendencies for youth to accelerate the transition to adulthood due to perceptions of a foreshortened life expectancy (Burton et al., 1995).

In sum, there needs to be continued empirical attention to normative developmental processes among children in poverty. Whereas many social-emotional constructs may show similar associations among disadvantaged youth and others, researchers must remain cautious in generalizing mainstream tenets about salient developmental processes to ecocultural contexts that differ substantially from those which originally spawned them.

Expanding Perspectives on Influences and Outcomes: The Need for Interdisciplinary Research

Conceptions of Salient Protective and Vulnerability Factors. A critical tenet in the emerging field of developmental psychopathology is that expertise from other scientific disciplines can substantially enrich psychologists' understanding of fundamental processes of child development (Cicchetti, 1993; Sroufe & Rutter, 1984). This tenet is of particular relevance for psychologists seeking to understand adaptational processes among children in poverty, for input from other disciplines can help to fill in many gaps in major mainstream psychology conceptualizations.

Consider perspectives about salient protective forces. As indicated in previous discussions (Chapter 4), Baumrind's well-known typology of parenting behaviors does not operate among the poor as it does among the middle class: rather than democratic, authoritative behaviors, most adaptive in inner-cities are often those strategies reflecting high strictness and monitoring of children. Similarly, success at some of the classic developmental tasks of adolescence (e.g., doing well at school and getting along with peers) are not necessarily mutually facilitative, but can sometimes be mutually inhibitory within the setting of the inner city (Chapter 5).

In parallel fashion, some indices that are typically viewed as signs of psychiatric dysfunction do not invariably represent personal psychopathology among children in disadvantaged settings. Behaviors which psychologists might label as "conduct disordered," for example, are seen as highly adaptive for long-term survival by many youth growing up in crime-ridden, inner-city areas (Chapter 5). Similarly, out-of-wedlock, teen motherhood, generally perceived as a risk factor for diverse long-term outcomes, can carry several benefits in the minds of youth in poverty. For many inner-city girls, becoming a mother represents not only attaining the cherished status of adulthood, but also the potential gateway to several gratifying intimate relationships with her infant, the baby's father, and even his extended kin (Burton et al., 1995; Simon & Burns, 1997). Implicit in such evidence is the message that in future research, it is critical to consider not only mainstream views on salient risk and protective factors, but also the *people's own perceptions* of positive and negative ramifications of particular behaviors or outcomes (Cohler et al., 1995; Harwood et al., 1996).

For developmental psychologists committed to considering indigenous perspectives, there is much to be gained by drawing upon expertise from other social science disciplines, notably anthropology. Ethnographic research, the hallmark of anthropology, is generative, inductive, and centrally focused on *describing* salient processes in naturally occurring phenomena (LeCompte & Preissle, 1993). Insights gleaned from such qualititative research can be invaluable in facilitating the contextual relevance and thematic comprehensiveness of any quantitative studies, typically favored by psychologists, on risk and protective influences. Put simply, meaningful hypothesis-testing presupposes knowledge of the web of interrelated forces that can each underlie or affect the phenomenon under study. "We must understand how persons within a culture or ethnic group symbolically construct concepts such as self and others before we can understand factors attributed to vulnerability and resilience" (Cohler et al., 1995, p. 781).

Recent ethnographic studies involving poor families have illuminated several potentially important processes that merit further scrutiny in psychological research of a verificative or predictive nature. Jarrett (1995), for example, described diverse conceptions of "positive parenting" among low-income parents, some of which have been considered in prior quantitative studies (e.g., stringency of monitoring strategies) whereas others, such as the use of symbolic barriers to restrict relationships in the neighborhood, have received less attention. Similarly, based on interviews with inner-city families, Burton and colleagues' (1995) point to several aspects of adolescent adaptation that might promote long-term competence, each rarely considered in prior psychological research. These include contribution to cohesion at the family level and the community level (e.g., helping young mothers and elderly folk in the community) and development of creative talents in contextually relevant models (such as rapping or "doing hair and nails well").

In recent years, a few quantitative researchers have ventured toward harnessing the power inherent in interdisciplinary methodologies (e.g., Harwood et al., 1996). Exemplary in this regard is research by Brody and colleagues (1994) on salient intrafamilial processes among rural African American families, a study which evolved from a series of initial focus groups involving members of the local community. Participants of these groups helped the researchers pinpoint aspects of family functioning that were important versus irrelevant for individuals like themselves, and also helped finesse the wording of self-report instruments (e.g., by rephrasing items). In future research, strategies such as these can substantially enhance the power of empirical studies aimed at verifying, through quantitative measurement and data analyses, the contributions of major vulnerability and protective forces that affect the adjustment of children in poverty.

Maladjustment Versus Competence: Operational Definitions in Research. Accumulating ethnographic evidence on dissonance between subcultural and mainstream perspectives can beget dilemmas for developmental researchers vis-à-vis operationalizing child outcomes in the context of poverty. In designating a particular child behavior as maladaptive or otherwise, which viewpoint should be considered: the microcosmic or the macrocosmic? In general, absolutism is inadvisable, and researchers should consider associated losses *and* gains of the behavior in question. To illustrate, Jarrett (1990) has shown that in many childhood games, nondelinquent aggressive behaviors, such as mutual verbal attacks in contest format ("rippin"), can substantially bolster solidarity within the peer group—an important source of support and self-esteem for children with limited family resources. Such aggressive behaviors do not, therefore, unequivocally represent externalizing psychopathology; they may also often be appropriately treated as positive indices serving the important functional necessity of promoting peer group solidarity (Luthar, 1997; Prinz & Miller, 1991).

Obviously, such an "impartial" stance in research is warranted only to the degree that the behavior in question does not have any negative ramifications that are extreme. Thus, although membership in a criminal inner-city gang might foster short-term feelings of peer group solidarity, to view this as an adaptive outcome over the long term would be ludicrous given the real dangers the child himself faces as well as his potential to seriously harm others. There is little adaptive about long-term incarceration, leave alone violent death.

As with defining maladjustment, investigators may often face dilemmas in selecting among contradictory perspectives while operationalizing child competence, and in this case, optimal choices lie in those outcomes that reflect relative resonance with *both* microsystemic and macrosystemic mores (Luthar & Burack, in press). Without doubt, it is critical that developmental researchers recognize and take seriously what poor children themselves see as reflecting successful adaptation. On the other hand, it may be most profitable to conceive of a hierarchy of competence outcomes, wherein youngsters who succeed according to one set of societal rules but clearly fail according to another are not rated quite as positively as those who seem to have negotiated, fairly successfully, both worlds they live in—the microcosm of the immediate subculture and the macrocosm of wider society which encompasses it. These apparently "bicultural" youth (e.g., Phinney, 1990; Spencer & Markstron-Adams, 1990) appear to retain many of the major rewards of the immediate subculture as well as wider society, exemplified by students in inner-city schools who maintain high academic grades, and at the same time, are well appreciated and respected by their peers (Luthar & McMahon, 1996).

Other Interdisciplinary Collaborations. Returning to the issue of cross-discipline collaborations: in addition to anthropology, expertise from several other disciplines can substantially augment developmental psychologists' efforts to understand risk and protective processes among poor children. Of special relevance is epidemiology. Among the investigations reviewed in this volume, most of those involving children past the preschool years were school-based. There are obvious advantages to school-based sampling: it does capture the majority of targeted children given laws regarding compulsory school attendance and is also logistically attractive, permitting resources to be focused on in-depth examination of psychological processes. On the other hand is the obvious pitfall in using what have been called samples of convenience (O'Connor & Rutter, 1996), that is, some of the most vulnerable youth can be missed.[1] Incompleteness in sampling could not only result in underestimations of links between poverty and adjustment problems, but could also leave little learned about deleterious and beneficial forces that might uniquely affect the most vulnerable of poor children.

Even as we continue in-depth study of psychosocial processes in school-based studies, there is much value in also examining developmental processes within epidemiological samples. Although families from the lowest SES groups may once again be overrepresented among refusals to participate (Verhulst & Koot, 1992), as O'Connor and Rutter (1996) have noted, the representativeness of the sample is the *sine qua non* of epidemiological research. Concerted attempts to bring developmental expertise to the sampling rigor of epidemiology (e.g., Kellam, 1987; Rutter, 1989b) can thus be invaluable in promoting a more complete understanding of processes that shape the life trajectories of poor youth.

Also of value would be more research collaborations between developmental psychologists and professionals who interface intimately with subgroups of poor youth at particularly high psychiatric risk, such as social workers, child psychiatrists, and clinical psychologists. There have been few empirical attempts to examine developmental processes among children in inpatient psychiatric facilities, for example, or in juvenile detentions, both settings in which poor youth are highly overrepresented. To illustrate, statistics from the children's psychiatric inpatient unit at the Yale New Haven Hospital showed that between 1992 and 1997, approximately six of every ten admissions were children from families receiving financial assistance from the state. By contrast, in the general population, the proportion of families on Medicaid during this period was less than two of ten (J. W. Woolston, personal communication, December 9, 1997).

Again, there is much to be learned about vulnerability processes among poor youth who develop serious forms of psychopathology, that is, children with major psychiatric diagnoses and not just those with high scores on symptom check lists. As much research in child psychiatry has shown, the causal processes which eventuate in psychopathology within the normal ranges can be quite different from those operating at the extremes of clinical dysfunction (Cantwell & Rutter, 1994; O'Connor & Rutter, 1996).

The value of collaborations between developmental psychologists and behavioral geneticists has already been noted in previous discussions (Chapter 4). Such collaborative ventures have great potential to fine-tune our understanding of the environmental versus genetic components underlying links between parental psychopathology indices and child maladjustment, specifically within the context of disenfranchised, economically impoverished life circumstances.

Finally, there is a need for greater consideration of ways in which biological and neuropsychological processes might interact with psychological ones, in the development of psychopathology among poor youth. Several streams of evidence attest to the value of this work. Relevant, for example, are research findings on the possible role of disturbances in cognitive processes, language, speech, and motor coordination, in the ontogenesis of conduct disorders (Kazdin, 1995; Moffitt, 1993b). Also relevant are data showing that children in poverty are particularly vulnerable to many such problems. Infants born to poor women are at heightened risk for prematurity, low birthweight, and congenital anomalies, as well as developmental delays and neuropsychological deficits. Poverty is highly correlated with at least two major causes of brain dysfunction, head injuries (accidental or intentional) and exposure to lead (National Research Council, 1993), and recent research on brain development has shown that by 18 months of age, children raised in poor environments may already exhibit cognitive deficits of substantial magnitude (Carnegie Corporation, 1994). Data such as these collectively underscore the need for greater empirical attention to ways in which biological risks might interact with psychosocial forces in influencing the long term adjustment of children in poverty.

Effect Sizes and Data Analyses

Any concerted commentary on the magnitude of links involving poverty and child outcomes was precluded in this book, given the central objective of integrating an extensive literature on risk and protective processes. Nevertheless, at least a brief appraisal of this issue seems in order, since the merits of any future research on factors that modify the risks of poverty rest on the assumption that poverty does, in fact, have nontrivial effects on children.

Effect sizes of poverty have frequently been discussed in terms of links between family income and child outcomes (see Duncan & Brooks-Gunn, 1997a; Mayer, 1997), and literature reviews have indicated consistent but modest effects for income (and for other demographic indices considered individually) (Achenbach, Verhulst, Baron, & Akkerhuis, 1987; Loeber & Dishion, 1983). Inferences about the "unique" effects of low family income typically derive from studies involving multivariate data analyses, with statistical controls for other variables that typically co-occur with it such as large family size, parents' education, and life in resource-poor neighborhoods.

Although such multivariate analyses can be useful—they can help gauge the potential value of cash transfers (see Duncan & Brooks-Gunn, 1997a)—it is unwise to view small coefficients as indicating that "money does not matter," for the very factors that coexist with low income in the real world are forced to compete with it within the statistical analyses. Rutter has written about the pitfalls of interpreting such analyses too literally, emphasizing that when risk factors co-occur in reality, statistical controls for other factors do *not* reveal the effects of a particular risk operating in isolation (O'Connor & Rutter, 1996; Rutter, 1990). In a similar vein, Bronfenbrenner (as cited in Steinberg, Darling, Fletcher, Brown, & Dornbusch, 1995) has argued that it is meaningless to statistically control for ethnicity, social class, or household structure in efforts to isolate "pure" effects of a particular construct. Each of these processes occurs within a context, and understanding context necessitates taking it into account, and not trying to control it away.

What, however, of the modest effect sizes that have been indicated for socioeconomic indices in *univariate* associations, when co-occurring risks are not partialled away? Rowe and Rogers (1998) note that even simple, zero-order correlations between such indices and child outcomes are rarely greater than 0.30 to 0.35. These authors argue that much of the variance unexplained by poverty indices reflects genetic influences on child maladjustment, an argument difficult to categorically dispute in the face of a growing body of supporting evidence (e.g., Plomin, 1994; 1995). To persist with the theme of apparently modest environmental effects of family poverty, however, three issues may be relevant vis-à-vis the size of links previously found.

First, associations involving poverty are typically nonlinear (Rogler, 1996), with substantial risks reflected by very poor children but not necessarily those close to the poverty line. Epidemiological data from the Great Smoky Mountains Study (Costello et al., 1996) showed that the poorest children were at an approximately threefold greater risk than others for at least one lifetime psychiatric disorder. By contrast, with even modestly higher family income levels, differences with children in the highest income groups were attenuated. In short, beyond the threshold of average income levels, affluence may buy little in terms of child outcomes (Felner et al., 1995).[2]

Second, few would argue that family income alone is critical in influencing child outcomes. In point of fact, several studies (see Chapter 4) reflect the theme that whereas single risks may matter little, children's vulnerability increases exponentially with increasing numbers of risks that are *typically linked with low income*. Returning to the issue of effect sizes, then, one might argue that in future research, the significance of income should be gauged not only in terms of its own correlations with child outcomes but also in terms of correlations involving other variables with which it usually co-occurs in the real world. As Hauser and Sweeney (1997) caution, "Whatever its sources, a narrow focus on economic resources may not be scientifically valid. . . . Overly economist thinking may have diverted researchers from other major sources, dimensions, and consequences of social inequality" (p. 575). Stated differently, in future studies, the simultaneous consideration of several indices, each commonly associated with economic deprivation, is likely to be the most comprehensive measure of the total psychosocial adversity experienced by children in poverty (Entwisle & Astone, 1994; Hauser, 1994).

Third, from a data analytic perspective, a related issue—again involving the appraisal of gestalts rather than isolated variables—involves consideration of multiple child outcomes. In future research on risk and protective processes, there needs to be greater attention to children's overall adjustment profiles using individual-based data analyses (Magnusson & Bergman, 1988), in addition to the variable-based ones that have more typically been used. Person-based appraisals can be invaluable in helping to forestall hasty conclusions about "across-the-board" competence among disadvantaged children, simply on the basis of correlational data involving one or two relatively circumscribed variables (Luthar, 1997). Furthermore, children exposed to serious disadvantage may often show only moderate elevations in individual symptom areas (e.g., depression or conduct problems); yet, the true extent of damage to them may be evident in the coexistence of multiple forms of disturbance or "syndromes" of dysfunction (Fergusson et al., 1994; Fergusson & Lynskey, 1996). Disturbances in adjustment often gravitate to small clusters of individuals with multiple problems (e.g., delinquent behaviors, alcohol abuse, and drug abuse), and it often is the accumulation of adjustment problems, rather than the occurrence of individual symptoms, that can carry the greatest predictive significance for future maladjustment (Stattin & Magnusson, 1996). Obviously, there is much to be gained by more research on factors that eventuate in such profiles of multiple psychiatric difficulties among children growing up in poverty.

Research Designs: Comparison Groups and Longitudinal Studies

Although research on nonmainstream children has sometimes been criticized if it does not involve comparison groups (see Graham, 1992; Hobfoll et al., 1995), there is no correct or incorrect strategy here: decisions to include comparison groups must be dictated by the research question at hand. If the objective were to document the magnitude of links between low SES and negative developmental outcomes, a large, socioeconomically heterogenous sample would clearly be necessary. On the other hand, when research involves samples that are unquestionably at high risk (e.g., children facing chronic poverty along with serious parental psychopathology) there is obvious value in *within group* analyses focused on identifying processes which might mitigate the effects of the risks in question (e.g., Luthar et al., 1998; Quinton, Rutter, & Gulliver, 1990). As Hobfoll and colleagues (1995) have noted, requiring comparison groups in research involving any group of at-risk children would double the size, expense, and taxing of resources in studying vulnerability and protective factors among youngsters facing extreme adversities.

Issues of resource utilization are also relevant in weighing the relative merits of expensive longitudinal research designs that span extended periods of time. Repeated assessments of poor families and children across several years can certainly be valuable in illuminating potentially bidirectional casual associations. To illustrate, they can help to clarify cause-effect links between parents' psychopathology and their earning potential; or the degree to which chronic community violence results in high levels of aggression among youth as opposed to the converse.

In reality, many such associations are at least partly reciprocal or mutually deleterious in nature, and the scientific gains achieved by precisely quantifying each cause-effect association in "pure" research must be weighed against the benefits of bringing some of the same resources to applied research efforts. In the last several decades, psychologists' attempts to understand salient factors in poor children's adjustment have far outstripped their efforts to *apply* accumulating knowledge in rigorous intervention research. And as will be argued in the following section, carefully designed, research-based interventions have the potential not only to improve the life circumstances of poor children, but also to further our understanding of etiological processes—by indicating the degree to which changes across diverse areas of risk or protection do, in fact, result in improvements within particular areas of children's adjustment (Reynolds, 1998).

INTERVENTIONS

In preceding chapters, discussions on processes underlying individual vulnerability and protective factors frequently included associated implications for intervening within discrete domains. Moving away from analyses of particular influences, what are the broader messages that derive for interventions and social policy?

Perhaps the most conspicuous message is that efforts to improve poor children's well-being must necessarily be multipronged, targeting not just children themselves but also facets of communities and families. Poverty affects children's mental health not only directly by eroding their personal coping resources and feelings of well-being, but also via disturbances that reverberate throughout their surrounding environs of home and family, school and peers, and neighborhood and wider community. Furthermore, problems developing within any one of these spheres often galvanize downward spirals in others contiguously related.

Collectively, these factors point to the inadequacy of conventional, single-system treatment models which offer time-delimited intervention in relative isolation from the daily contexts of children's lives (e.g., individual psychotherapy targeting particular presenting symptoms). Undoubtedly, many such treatments may often serve more affluent youth well. Among poor children as well as the adults charged with their care, however, efforts to reduce any maladaptive behaviors require concerted and ongoing attention to the contextual and historical forces that contribute to their inception and/or continuity. Restated in more concrete terms, treatments targeting particular child symptoms or indices of well-being can achieve only limited success unless significant adults in the child's life space are involved in integral ways (Conduct Problems Prevention Research Group, 1992; Knitzer, in press). By the same token, the success of interventions for poor mothers (e.g., targeting parenting behaviors, substance use, or employability) will inevitably be constrained as long as the mothers themselves continue to be overwhelmed by feelings of depression, hopelessness, powerlessness, and social isolation (Luthar & Suchman, in press; Seitz, in press).

Supplementing these arguments against the neglect of significant others are the substantial advantages of their systematic *inclusion* in interventions. Poor families and communities have the potential to provide prodigious support for their own, and their ongoing involvement in designing and implementing interventions can be critical in maintaining the long-term gains of beneficial programs. Thus, there is much to commend intervention efforts which go beyond providing specific mental health services, and simultaneously work at strengthening, over time, the health-promoting capacities of salient components in poor children's surrounds: their families, schools, neighborhoods, and community clinics.

Collaborative participation of local community members—concerned and responsible parents, teachers, clinicians, as well the children themselves—can also bolster the resonance of intervention themes with major subcultural beliefs and values. Input from these individuals can help not only to ensure that identified intervention goals will be viewed as personally meaningful by intended recipients, but also to guide intervention staff toward therapeutic techniques likely to be most effective within that particular subculture (e.g., Brody et al., 1994; Cowen et al., 1996; Seitz, in press).

Proposals for multifaceted interventions for poor children might invoke, for some, fears of great strains on the nation's fiscal resources; yet, such apprehensions can be ill-founded for several reasons. First, preventive services are frequently not only more effective but also more cost-effective than remedial ones. Investments in the well-being of today's children in poverty can substantially promote their potential to become gainfully employed, productive members of society, as opposed to remaining debilitated, as adults, by social-emotional difficulties that become increasingly well-entrenched over the years. Research reviews have indicated, in fact, that early intervention programs which have used ecological, family-oriented designs, providing diverse components including skills-development and emotional support for both poor children and their parents, have led to reduced risk for various long-term negative outcomes including welfare dependency and criminal involvement (Seitz, in press; Yoshikawa, 1994).

Additionally, there are many ways in which largely untapped resources that currently exist in poor communities can be brought to bear within multi-pronged interventions. A range of possibilities in this regard are evident within Zigler's "School of the 21st Century," a comprehensive, model program that is built into existing public school systems. In this program, public school buildings, which remain unoccupied for large portions of the day and the calendar year, are used not only to house child care programs for children three years and older, but also to host regular support group meetings for parents. The program includes a strong outreach component: Information and referral networks are developed in schools to help families make better use of various existing services scattered across their communities, such as those offering counseling, physical health care, or night care for children. Finally, schools serve as hubs for child care, not only providing on-site care for children over 3 years of age (between 7 a.m. and 6 p.m.), but also coordinating and organizing community family day care facilities for children less than 3 years of age. The substantial promise of this program lies, conjointly, in its mobilization of existing community resources, in its potential to fill major service needs of providing quality child care for poor mothers—increasingly required to join the work force—and in the high level of success demonstrated by several projects initiated across various parts of the country (see Zigler & Gilman, 1996).

Other Exemplars

Increasingly over the years, interventionists have moved toward involving both families and communities in attempting to foster positive adjustment outcomes among poor youth (Knitzer, 1996). Two illustrations of such programs are provided in this section, one targeting preschool children and the other, school age youth.

Before discussing the programs in question, a word of clarification is necessary regarding reasons for their inclusion here. Specific programs are briefly described in order to provide concrete illustrations of some ways in which families and communities might be involved in interventions, as well as the potential benefits of such involvement. Using two particular programs for such illustrative purposes does not imply that future interventionists should necessarily replicate all facets of these, or that all aspects have unequivocally been endorsed as equally beneficial by the scientific community (see Natriello, McDill, & Pallas, 1990). Rather, concrete examples are provided toward the broader goal of considering how principles of family and community involvement might most effectively be translated into the design of future intervention programs.

The Perry Preschool Project, among the most influential in the area of early childhood interventions,[3] was implemented in Ypsilanti, Michigan, during the 1960s. This intervention was designed to serve low-income, African American preschoolers thought to be at risk for intellectual and academic difficulties. The project involved random assignment of over 100 children between 3 and 4 years of age to a preschool intervention or a control group.

The preschool group received high quality, cognitively oriented, early childhood intervention for one to two academic years. Apart from activities directly promoting educational enrichment and school readiness, the program also had a strong parent outreach component. Teachers made weekly home visits to inform parents about their children's activities and educational progress, and monthly small group meetings were held during which parents could share perspectives on child-rearing and exchange support for each other's changing perspectives in this regard.

Longitudinal data have shown that program graduates reflected several advantages over comparison youth who did not receive the preschool intervention (Berrueta-Clement, Schweinhart, Barnett, Epstein, & Weikart, 1984; Schweinhart, Barnes, & Weikart, 1993). At age 19, for example, the intervention group showed better high school graduation rates (67% versus 49%), and higher standardized achievement test scores. They were also less likely to engage in crime: only 31% of preschool group members had been arrested or charged at least once, compared to 51% of control group. At age 27, program participants had significantly higher earnings, and among the women, were more likely to be married and less likely to have borne children outside of marriage. Again, criminal involvement was significantly lower at age 27, as indexed, for example, by differences in average arrest rates.

The Perry Preschool Program has proved to be cost-effective as well. By the time participants had reached 19 years of age, reductions in costs related to delinquency and crime were estimated to be approximately $2,400 per child. By the 27-year follow-up, estimates were that the preschool intervention had saved approximately $7 for every dollar invested (Barnett, 1993).

The School Development Project of New Haven, Connecticut is another exemplar of community- and family-based interventions that enhance the well-being of children in poverty (Comer, 1988; Haynes & Comer, 1996). This program, conceived to improve both educational and social-emotional outcomes among elementary school children in inner-cities, involves efforts to rebuild learning communities by connecting various significant adults in children's lives. A central component of the intervention is the "school planning and management team," a governance body comprising of not only the school principal, teachers, and support staff, but also, parents and students themselves, as well as members of the wider community. This team is charged with the responsibility of setting the overall agenda for the school and for shaping its social and academic climate.

Two other critical components are the "student and staff support team" and the "parent program," both of which involve trained professionals with experience in child mental health and school-related problems. The first of these teams works with students and staff to prevent potential problem situations from developing into crises. The second involves parents at various levels: by including them in school-sponsored social activities, recruiting them to work collaboratively with school staff, and involving them in the school planning team. Community involvement, similarly, is bi-directional in nature. Community groups bring needed resources to children in the schools, and school personnel travel out to the community to provide services as well as to learn. Across all levels of this program, there is an ongoing and explicit emphasis on ensuring a climate of respect, openness, and trust in the interventionists' work with students, teachers, parents, and community members.

Studies on the effects of this venture have suggested various benefits including improvements in students' achievement and overall adjustment, teachers' feelings of efficacy and satisfaction, and parents' feelings of connectedness with the schools as well as, frequently, their resumed schooling and/or pursuit of meaningful work (see Haynes & Comer, 1996, for a review). Aside from gains in these individual areas, among the most attractive features of this program is its potential to sustain itself. Summarizing some of his earliest efforts in New Haven schools, Comer wrote, "In 1980 our group left the schools. The program was fully integrated into the normal practices of the staff, who continued to carry it out. . . . We left intact the key elements of our success in New Haven—the governance and management team, the parents program, and the mental health team, along with our operating rules—while allowing specific social and academic activities to vary with the needs of a particular school." (1988, p. 48). The most valuable legacy of programs such as this, then, may lie in their capacities to empower seriously disenfranchised communities to set into motion working systems, whereby they gradually come to depend on their own growing skills and capacities to provide optimal environments for their developing young.

A final comment on intervention directions: there is a need not only for the development of conceptually sound, ecologically valid, and logistically feasible interventions for poor youth, but also for their systematic grounding in empirical research (Knitzer, 1996). To maximize the gains from initially promising programs, their techniques and procedures must be documented in detail within treatment manuals to allow for subsequent replication of their effects and their eventual dissemination across other similar sites (Kazdin, 1995). Also indispensable are rigorous assessments of outcomes and process in randomized research designs, as in the recently begun FAST Track program (Conduct Problems Prevention Research Group, 1992). Assessment packages must be carefully designed so that they can capture salient areas of improvement (and deterioration) among program recipients as compared to nonrecipients, both at post-intervention as well as several months subsequently. In addition, these measurement batteries should have the potential to illuminate intervening processes which can, in conceptually satisfactory ways, explain or account for salient improvements that are evidenced by program recipients.

TEACHING AND CURRICULA

The concluding section of this chapter is devoted to directions for training future students for work on child development in the context of poverty. Given the ways in which academic training is currently structured, there are four major issues considered. The first of these is that there remains a distressing lack of diversity in child development instructional curricula (Luthar, 1997). Whereas in the past, such gaps might have been attributable to a dearth of sophisticated research on non-mainstream children (see Graham, 1992), this argument, as amply indicated by the accumulated wealth of evidence reviewed in this volume, is no longer tenable. There is a critical need to bring research on issues facing poor families and children into mainstream child development, by including these in both undergraduate and graduate teaching curricula and by ensuring their representation in major textbooks (Spencer, 1988).

The second need is for more efforts at cross-disciplinary training. For students aspiring to both scholarship and practice, there is much to be gained from first-hand exposure to perspectives of various professionals interfacing with different facets of poor children's life experiences (Knitzer, 1996): social workers, community mental health workers, teachers and school administrators, policy makers, law enforcement officials, and social science researchers (both quantitative and qualitative). Each of these groups of individuals can provide valuable and unique insights into the complex web of processes that are implicated in disadvantaged children's adjustment.

The third issue, related though less frequently noted, is that vignettes and narratives can be invaluable pedagogical supplements to formal instructional materials in sensitizing students to issues facing poor families (Jarrett, 1994). In a persuasive article, Schnitzer (1996) argued that stories can be invaluable in helping clinical students to see beyond what may seem like poor parents' apathy or resistance to psychotherapy treatments, vividly illuminating the surfeit of obstacles that they must surmount to attend treatment sessions. For many poor parents, these include forced reliance on erratic and highly inconvenient public transportation systems and ongoing difficulties in securing child care for their youngest, tangible pressures that are compounded (as indicated at the outset of this chapter) by years of exposure to negative judgmental reactions from "service providers."

Personal vignettes can be beneficial not only for clinical trainees but also for aspiring researchers, as they can heighten students' comprehension of the assorted challenges confronting poor families and in turn, enhance the sensitivity of their research. As Cohler, Stott, and Musick (1995) have argued, narratives of at-risk individuals' life stories can be invaluable in helping students grasp the ways in which day-to-day difficulties interface with major misfortune in determining threats to present adjustment. Without compromising at all our commitment to rigorous empiricism, therefore, there can be value in also including, in our premier publications of child development research, narratives that vivify the issues addressed. Doing this has the potential not only to inspire more talented investigators to work in the area, but also to guide them to new, unexplored research hypotheses about critical risk and protective processes implicated in poor children's adjustment.

The fourth issue concerning future training needs involves presentation of research data. Students need to learn to effectively convey their findings not only to others in science, but also to the general public, as well as, most importantly, to policy makers. There needs to be more emphasis in graduate training on presenting research findings concisely and in jargon-free language, with the life circumstances of poor children captured in three-dimensional, humanized terms rather than simply with diagnostic labels and statistical effect sizes (Huston, 1994b; Knitzer, 1996). In addition, there is a need to capture messages in a comprehensive way without sounding equivocal on what the substantive message is. Whereas psychologists are trained to carefully consider rival hypotheses via relevant data, policy makers need concise summaries of the facts. Highlighting this difference, Edward Zigler (1993, p. 11) thus described a congressman's response to a researcher's presentation: "What this country needs is a one-armed psychologist. You guys are always saying "on the one hand. . .but on the other hand. . . .""

SUMMARY

1. To effectively guide future research on risk and protective processes affecting poor children, there is a need to refine conceptual models on normative child development in the context of poverty. This can often be accomplished by extending classic developmental theories, according centrality to themes that are unique and powerful in the lives of poor children. As for any evolving science, contributions can derive not only from grand theories of development, but also more circumscribed theories of the mid-range.

2. In terms of research directions for the future, apart from pursuing unanswered questions regarding particular risk and protective factors (summarized in preceding chapters of this book), there is value in more research on normative developmental processes in the context of poverty. Also needed is greater empirical attention to definitions of, and pathways to, both competence and maladjustment, as they are defined indigenously and not just by mainstream psychology. Developmental psychologists' efforts to understand risk and protective mechanisms would be greatly enhanced by more interdisciplinary collaborations with anthropologists and sociologists, as well as with epidemiologists, social workers, child psychiatrists, and those with expertise in genetic, biological and neuropsychological factors in children's social-emotional adjustment.

The issue of effect sizes involving poverty and child outcomes should be approached not just in terms of single indices such as income, but also in terms of the many other risks that typically co-occur with low income. There is also value in a greater use of individual-based data analyses examining children's overall profiles in addition to variable-based ones involving individual domains.

Comparison groups in studies on poor children are obviously critical when examining effect sizes of poverty. Conversely, in studying modifiers of risk *within* multiply disadvantaged samples, it is more difficult to justify the additional resources needed to include mainstream comparison groups. Similarly, the scientific gains of resource-intensive, "pure" longitudinal research must be weighed against the benefits that can derive from applying some of these resources to preventive or remedial interventions which have a strong basis in scientific research.

3. For interventions targeting poor children's well-being, it is vital that family and community members are integrally involved in both the planning and implementation of treatments. Of greatest ultimate value are ecologically

grounded, multifaceted interventions which in addition to providing particular services to foster children's well-being, help disenfranchised communities develop their own health-promoting capacities. By the same token, there can be limited effectiveness, at best, to any efforts that involve one-shot, single-system services provided to children, divorced from the challenges and contexts of their daily lives.

4. Finally, there is a need for greater diversity of curricula in educating future scholars concerned with poverty and child development. Narratives about the lives of poor children and families can be a helpful supplement to formal instructional materials, in vividly conveying the realities of life in poverty—of which many might otherwise remain only faintly aware. In addition, students should be prepared in ways to effectively communicate research findings not only to peers in science but also to policy makers, an audience who can be strongly influenced by research data and in turn, can substantially affect the life circumstances of thousands of poor children living in poverty.

NOTES

1. Such omissions can occur not only because of parents' refusals to participate or high drop-out rates among older youth, but also because of high absenteeism due to temporary placements in juvenile detentions, emergency foster homes, homeless shelters, and psychiatric hospitals—all settings in poor youth are disproportionately represented.

2. There is also evidence that on some indices, notably adolescent substance use, falling in the *highest* of income brackets can reflect levels of risk that are at least commensurate with, if not greater than, those at low-SES levels (National Adolescent Health Resource Center, 1996).

3. Head Start is another highly influential, multifaceted early intervention program, involving early childhood education along with health care for children, social services for both child and family, and a high emphasis on parent involvement. Research evaluations of Head Start, however, have focused overwhelmingly on children's gains in IQ and cognitive achievement; there is relatively little systematic information on long-term gains in participants' psychological and social adjustment (Zigler & Styfco, 1996).

REFERENCES

Adler, N. E., Boyce, T., Chesney, M. A., Cohen, S., Folkman, S., Kahn, R. L., & Syme, S. L. (1994). Socioeconomic status and health. The challenge of the gradient. *American Psychologist, 49,* 1524.

Allen, J. P., Leadbeater, B. J., Aber, J. L. (1994). The development of problem behavior syndromes in at-risk adolescents. *Development & Psychopathology, 6,* 323-342.

Allen, L., Denner, J., Yoshikawa, H., Seidman, E., & Aber, J. L. (1996). Acculturation and depression among Latina urban girls. In B. J. Leadbeater & J. Way (Eds.), *Urban girls: Resisting stereotypes, creating identities* (pp. 337-352). New York: New York University Press.

Allison, D. (1996). *Two or three things I know for sure.* New York: Plume.

Alpern, L., & Lyons-Ruth, K. (1993). Preschool children at social risk: Chronicity and timing of maternal depressive symptoms and child behavior problems at school and at home. *Development & Psychopathology, 5,* 371-387.

Apfel, N., & Seitz, V. (1996). African-American adolescent mothers, their families, and their daughters: A longitudinal perspective over twelve years. In B. J. Leadbeater & N. Way (Eds.), *Urban girls: Resisting stereotypes, creating identities* (pp. 149-170).New York: New York University Press.

Apfel, N., & Seitz, V. (1997). The firstborn sons of African-American teenage mothers: Perspectives on risk and resilience. In S. S. Luthar, J. A. Burack, D. Cicchetti, & J. R. Weisz, (Eds.), *Developmental psychopathology: Perspectives on adjustment, risk, and disorder* (pp. 486-506). New York: Cambridge.

Arroyo, C. G., & Zigler, E. (1995). Racial identity, academic achievement, and the psychological well-being of economically disadvantaged adolescents. *Journal of Personality and Social Psychology, 69,* 903-914.

Attar, B. K., Guerra, N. G., & Tolan, P. H. (1994). Neighborhood disadvantage, stressful life events, and adjustment in urban elementary school children. *Journal of Clinical Child Psychology, 23,* 391-400.

Azuma, S. D., & Chasnoff, I. J. (1993). Outcome of children prenatally exposed to cocaine and other drugs: A path analysis of three-year data. *Pediatrics, 92,* 396-402.

Baldwin, A. L., Baldwin, C., & Cole, R. E. (1990). Stress-resistant families and stress-resistant children. In J. Rolf, A. S. Masten, D. Cicchetti, K. H. Nuechterlein, & S. Weintraub (Eds.), *Risk and protective factors in the development of psychopathology* (pp. 257-280). New York: Cambridge.

Baldwin, A. L., Baldwin, C. P., Kasser, T., Zax, M., Sameroff, A., & Seifer, R. (1993). Contextual risk and resiliency during late adolescence. *Development & Psychopathology, 5,* 741-761.

Barnett, W. S. (1993). Cost-benefit analysis. In L. J. Schweinhart, H. V. Barnes, & D. P. Weikart (Eds.), *Significant benefits: The High/Scope Perry Preschool Study through age 27* (pp. 142-173). Ypsilanti, MI: High/Scope.

Baugher, E., & Lamison-White, L. (1996). *U.S. Bureau of the Census, Current Population Reports, Series P60-194, Poverty in the United States: 1995.* Washington, DC: Government Printing Office.

Baumrind, D. (1972). An exploratory study of socialization effects on Black children: Some Black-White comparisons. *Child Development, 43, 261-267.*

Belluck, P. (1997, September 9). Tribes new power over welfare may come at too high a price. *New York Times,* p. A1.

Belsky, J. (1980). Child maltreatment. An ecological integration. *American Psychologist, 35,* 320-335.

Belsky, J. (1984). The determinants of parenting: A process model. *Child Development, 55,* 83-96.

Berman, S. L., Kurtines, W. M., Silverman, W. K., & Serafini, L. T. (1996). The impact of exposure to crime and violence on urban youth. *American Journal of Orthopsychiatry, 66,* 329-336.

Berrueta-Clement, J. R., Schweinhart, L. J., Barnett, W. S., Epstein, A. S., & Weikart, D. P. (1984). *Changed lives: The effects of the Perry Preschool Program on youths through age 19.* Ypsilanti, MI: High/Scope.

Bettes, B. A., Dusenbury, L., Kerner, J., James-Ortiz, S., & Botvin, G. J. (1990). Ethnicity and psychosocial factors in alcohol and tobacco use in adolescence. *Child Development, 61,* 557-565.

Block, J. H., & Block, J. (1980). The role of ego-control and ego-resiliency in the organization of behavior. In W. A. Collins (Ed.), *Minnesota Symposium on Child Psychology: Vol. 13. Development of cognition, affect, and social relations* (pp. 39-101). Hillsdale, NJ: Erlbaum.

Bolger, K. E., Patterson, C. J., Thompson, W. W., & Kupersmidt, J. B. (1995). Psychosocial adjustment among children experiencing persistent and intermittent family economic hardship. *Child Development, 66,* 1107-1129.

Bowman, P. J. (1990). The adolescent-to adult transition: Discouragement among jobless black youth. In V. C. McLoyd & C. A. Flanagan (Eds.), *New Directions for Child Development: Vol. 46. Economic stress: Effects on family life and child development* (pp. 87-105). San Francisco: Jossey Bass.

Boxill, N. A., & Beaty, A. L. (1990). Mother/child interaction among homeless women and their children in a public night shelter in Atlanta, Georgia. *Child and Youth Services, 14,* 49-64.

Brody, G. H., Stoneman., Z., & Flor, D. (1996). Parental religiosity, family processes, and youth competence in rural, two-parent African American families. *Developmental Psychology, 32,* 696-706

Brody, G. H., Stoneman, Z., Flor, D., McCrary, C., Hastings, L., & Conyers, O. (1994). Financial resources, parent psychological functioning, parent co-caregiving, and early adolescent competence in rural two-parent African-American families. *Child Development, 65,* 590-605.

Bronfenbrenner, U. (1986). Ecology of the family as a context for human development: Research perspectives. *Developmental Psychology, 22,* 723-742.

Brooks-Gunn, J. (1995). Children in families and communities: Risk and intervention in the Bronfenbrenner tradition. In P. Moen, G. H. Elder, & K. Luscher (Eds.), *Examining lives in context* (pp. 467-51). Washington, DC: American Psychological Association.

Brooks-Gunn, J., & Chase-Lansdale, P. L. (1995). Adolescent parenthood. In M. H. Bornstein (Ed.), *Handbook of Parenting: Vol. 3. Status and social conditions of parenting* (pp. 113-150). Mahwah, NJ: Erlbaum.

Brooks-Gunn, J., & Furstenberg, F. F., Jr. (1987). Continuity and change in the context of poverty: Adolescent mothers and their children. In J. J. Gallagher & C. T. Ramey (Eds.), *The malleability of children* (pp. 171-188). Baltimore: Brookes.

Broman, C. L. (1996). Coping with personal problems. In H. W. Neighbors & J. S. Jackson (Eds.), *Mental health in Black America* (pp. 117-129). Thousand Oaks, CA: Sage.

Browne, A., & Bassuk, S. S. (1997). Intimate violence in the lives of homeless and poor housed women: Prevalence and patterns in an ethnically diverse sample. *American Journal of Orthopsychiatry, 67,* 261-278.

Brunswick, A., Lewis, C., & Messeri, P. (1991). A life span perspective on drug use and affective distress in an African-American sample. *Journal of Community Psychology, 19,* 123-135.

Burchinal, M. R., Follmer, A., & Bryant, D. M. (1996). The relations of maternal social support and family structure with maternal responsiveness and child outcomes among African-American families. *Developmental Psychology, 32,* 1073-1083.

Burton, L. (1990). Teenage childbearing as an alternative life-course strategy in multi-generation Black families. *Human Nature, 1,* 123-143.

Burton, L. M., Allison, K. W., & Obeidallah, D. (1995). Social context and adolescence: Perspectives on development among inner-city African-American teens. In L. J. Crockett & A. C. Crouter (Eds.), *Pathways through adolescence: Individual development in relation to social contexts* (pp. 119-138). Mahwah, NJ: Erlbaum.

Canino, I., Gould, M., Prupis, S., & Shaffer, D. (1986). A comparison of symptoms and diagnoses in Hispanic and Black children in an outpatient mental health clinic. *Journal of the American Academy of Child Psychiatry, 25,* 254-259.

Cantwell, D., & Rutter, M. (1994). Classification: Conceptual and substantive issues. In M. Rutter, E. Taylor, & L. Hersov (Eds.), *Child and adolescent psychiatry: Modern approaches* (3rd ed., pp. 3-21). Oxford, England: Blackwell Scientific.

Carnegie Corporation. (1994). *Starting points: Meeting the needs of our youngest children.* Carnegie Task Force. New York: Author.

Cauce, A. M. (1986). Social networks and social competence: Exploring the effects of early adolescent friendships. *American Journal of Community Psychology, 14,* 607-628.

Chaffin, M., Kelleher, K., & Hollenberg, J. (1996). Onset of physical abuse and neglect: Psychiatric, substance abuse, and social risk factors from prospective community data. *Child Abuse & Neglect, 20,* 191-203.

Chase-Lansdale, P. L., Brooks-Gunn, J., & Zamsky, E. S. (1994). Young African-American multigenerational families in poverty: Quality of mothering and grandmothering. *Child Development, 65*(2), 373-393.

Chase-Lansdale, P. L., & Gordon, R. A. (1996). Economic hardship and the development of five-and six-year olds: Neighborhood and regional perspectives. *Child Development, 67,* 3338-3367.

Chavez, E. L., Oetting, E. R., & Swaim, R. C. (1994). Dropout and delinquency: Mexican-American and Caucasian Non-Hispanic youth. *Journal of Clinical Child Psychology, 23,* 47-55.

Christoffel, K. K. (1997). Firearm injuries affecting U.S. children and adolescents. In J. D. Osofsky (Ed.), *Children in a violent society* (pp. 42-71). New York: Guilford.

Chute, C. (1985). *The beans of Egypt, Maine.* New York: Ticknor & Fields.

Cicchetti, D. (1993). Developmental psychopathology: Reactions, reflections, projections. *Developmental Review, 13,* 471502.

Cicchetti, D., & Lynch, M. (1995). Failures in the expectable environment and their impact on individual development: The case of child maltreatment. In D. Cicchetti & D. J. Cohen (Eds.), *Developmental psychopathology: Risk, disorder, and adaptation, Vol. 2.* (pp. 32-71). New York: Wiley.

Cicchetti, D., Rogosch, F. A., Lynch, M., & Holt, K. D. (1993). Resilience in maltreated children: Processes leading to adaptive outcomes. *Development & Psychopathology, 5,* 629-648.

Cicchetti, D., & Toth, S. L. (1995). Developmental psychopathology and disorders of affect. In D. Cicchetti & D. J. Cohen (Eds.), *Developmental psychopathology: Risk, disorder, and adaptation, Vol. 2.* (pp. 369-420). New York: Wiley.

Cohler, B. J., Stott, F. M., & Musick, J. S. (1995). Adversity, vulnerability, and resilience. Cultural and developmental perspectives. In D. Cicchetti, & D. J. Cohen (Eds.), *Developmental Psychopathology: Vol. 2. Risk, disorder and adaptation* (pp. 753-800). New York: Wiley.

Coie, J. D., Dodge, K. A., Terry, R., & Wright, V. (1990). The role of aggression in peer relations: An analysis of aggression episodes in boys' play groups. *Child Development, 62,* 812-826.

Coie, J. D., & Jacobs, M. R. (1993). The role of social context in the prevention of conduct disorder. *Development & Psychopathology, 5,* 263-275.

Coie, J. D., Terry, R., Lenox, K., Lockman, J., & Hyman, C. (1995). Childhood peer rejection and aggression as predictors of stable patterns of adolescent disorder. *Development & Psychopathology, 7,* 697-713.

Coie, J. D., Terry, R., Zakriski, A., & Lockman, J. (1995). Early adolescent social influences on delinquent behavior. In J. McCord (Ed.), *Coercion and punishment in long-term perspectives* (pp. 229-244). New York: Cambridge.

Comer, J. P. (1988). Educating poor minority children. *Scientific American, 259,* 42-48.

Conduct Problems Prevention Research Group. (1992). A developmental and clinical model for the prevention of conduct disorders: The Fast Track Program. *Development & Psychopathology, 4,* 509-527.

Conger, R. D., Conger, K. J., & Elder, G. H. (1997). Family economic hardship and adolescent adjustment: Mediating and moderating processes. In G. J. Duncan & J. Brooks-Gunn (Eds.), *Consequences of growing up poor* (pp. 288–310). New York: Russell Sage.

Conger, R. D., Ge, X., Elder, G. H., Lorenz, F. O., & Simons, R. L. (1994). Economic stress, coercive family process, and developmental problems of adolescents. *Child Development, 65,* 541-561.

Connell, J. P., Halpern-Felsher, B. L., Clifford, E., Crichlow, W., & Usinger, P. (1995). Hanging in there: Behavioral, psychological, and contextual factors affecting whether African American adolescents stay in high school. *Journal of Adolescent Research, 10,* 41-63.

Connell, J. P., Spencer, M. B., & Aber, J. L. (1994). Educational risk and resilience in African-American youth· Context, oolf, action, and outcomes in school. *Child Development, 65,* 493-506.

Costello, E. J., Angold, A., Burns, B. J., Stangl, D. K., Tweed, D. L., Erkanli, A., & Worthman, C. M. (1996). The Great Smoky Mountains Study of youth. *Archives of General Psychiatry, 53,* 1129-1136.

Costello, E. J., Farmer, M. Z., Angold, A., Burns, B. J., & Erkanli, A. (1997). Psychiatric disorders among American Indian and White youth in Appalachia: The Great Smoky Mountains Study. *American Journal of Public Health, 87,* 827-832.

Coulton, C. J., Korbin, J. E., So, M., & Chow, J. (1995). Community level factors and child maltreatment rates. *Child Development, 66,* 1262-1276.

Cowen, E. L., Hightower, A. D., Pedro-Carroll, J. L., Work, W. C., Wyman, P. A., & Haffrey, W. G. (1996). *School-based prevention for children at risk: The Primary Mental Health Project.* Washington, DC: American Psychological Association.

Cowen, E. L., Work, W. C., & Wyman, P. A. (1997). In S. S. Luthar, J. A. Burack, D. Cicchetti., & J. R. Weisz, (Eds.) *Developmental psychopathology: Perspectives on adjustment, risk, and disorder* (pp. 527-547). New York: Cambridge.

Crittenden, P. M. (1985). Maltreated infants: Vulnerability and resilience. *Journal of Child Psychology & Psychiatry, 26,* 85-96.

Cummings, E. M., & Davies, P. T. (1994). Maternal depression and child development. *Journal of Child Psychology and Psychiatry, 35,* 73-112.

Danziger, S., & Danziger, S. (1993). Child poverty and public policy: Toward a comprehensive antipoverty agenda. *Daedalus: America's Childhood, 122,* 57-84.

de Vries, M. W. (1984). Temperament and infant mortality among the Masai of East Africa. *American Journal of Psychiatry, 141,* 1189-1194.

de Cubas, M. M., & Field, T. (1993). Children of methadone-dependent women: Developmental outcomes. *American Journal of Orthopsychiatry, 63,* 266-276.

Dembo, R., Blount, W. R., Schmeidler, J., & Burgos, W. (1986). Perceived environmental drug use risk and the correlates of early drug use or nonuse among inner-city youths: The motivated actor. *International Journal of the Addictions, 21,* 977-1000.

DiBiase, R., & Waddell S. (1995). Some effects of homelessness on the psychological functioning of preschoolers. *Journal of Abnormal Child Psychology, 23,* 783-791.

Dishion, T. J., Andrews, D. W., & Crosby, L. (1995). Antisocial boys and their friends in early adolescence: Relationship characteristics, quality, and interactional process. *Child Development, 66,* 139-152.

Dodge, K. A., Coie, J. D., Pettit, G. S., & Price, J. M. (1990). Peer status and aggression in boys' groups: Developmental and contextual considerations. *Child Development, 61,* 1289-1309.

Dodge, K. A., Pettit, G. S., & Bates, J. E. (1994). Socialization mediators of the relation between socioeconomic status and child conduct problems. *Child Development, 65,* 649-665.

DuBois, D. L., Felner, R. D., Brand, S., Adan, A. M., & Evans, E. G. (1992). A prospective study of life stress, social support, and adaptation in early adolescence. *Child Development, 63,* 542-557.

DuBois, D. L., Felner, R. D., Meares, G., & Krier, M. (1994). Prospective investigation of the effects of socioeconomic disadvantage, life stress, and social support on early adolescent adjustment. *Journal of Abnormal Psychology, 103,* 511-522.

Dubow, E. F., Edwards, S., & Ippolito, M. F. (1997). Stress, neighborhood disadvantage, and resources: A focus on inner-city children's adjustment. *Journal of Clinical Child Psychology, 26,* 130-144.

Dumas, J. E., & Wekerle, C. (1995). Maternal reports of child behavior problems and personal distress as predictors of dysfunctional parenting. *Development & Psychopathology, 7,* 465-479.

Duncan, G. J. (1994). The economic environment of childhood. In A. C. Huston (Ed.), *Children in poverty* (pp. 23-50). New York: Cambridge.

Duncan, G. J., & Brooks-Gunn, J. (Eds.). (1997a). *Consequences of growing up poor.* New York: Russell Sage.

Duncan, G. J., & Brooks-Gunn, J. (1997b). Income effects across the life span: Integration and interpretation. In G. J. Duncan & J. Brooks-Gunn (Eds.), *Consequences of growing up poor* (pp. 541- 595). New York: Russell Sage.

Duncan, G. J., Brooks-Gunn, J., & Klebanov, P. K. (1994). Economic deprivation and early childhood development. *Child Development, 65,* 296-318.

Dunn, L. M., & Dunn, L. M. (1981). *Peabody Picture Vocabulary Test–Revised.* Circle Pines, MN: American Guidance Service.

DuRant, R. H., Getts, A., Cadenhead, C., Emans, S. J. & Woods, E. R. (1995). Exposure to violence and victimization and depression, hopelessness, and purpose in life among adolescents living in and around public housing. *Development & Behavioral Pediatrics, 16,* 233-237.

Eckenrode, J., Rowe, E., Laird, M., & Brathwaite, J. (1995). Mobility as a mediator of the effects of child maltreatment on academic performance. *Child Development, 66, 1130-1142.*

Egami, Y., Ford, D. E., Greenfield, S. F.,& Crum, R. M. (1996). Psychiatric profile and sociodemographic characteristics of adults who report physically abusing or neglecting children. *American Journal of Psychiatry, 153,* 921-928

Egeland, B., Carlson, E., & Sroufe, L. A. (1993). Resilience as process. *Development & Psychopathology, 5,* 517-528.

Egeland, B., & Kreutzer. (1991). A longitudinal study of the effects of maternal stress and protective factors on the development of high-risk children. In E. M. Cummings, A. L. Greene,& K. H. Karraker (Eds.), *Life-span developmental psychology: Perspectives on stress and coping* (pp. 61-84). Hillsdale, NJ: Erlbaum.

Egeland, B., & Sroufe, A. (1981). Developmental sequelae of maltreatment. In R. Rizley & D. Cicchetti (Eds.), *New directions for child development: Developmental perspectives in child maltreatment.* San Francisco: Jossey-Bass.

Elder, G. H. (1974). *Children of the Great Depression.* Chicago: University of Chicago Press.

Elder, G. H., Liker, J. K., & Cross, C. E. (1984). Parent-child behavior in the Great Depression: Life course and intergenerational influences. *Life Span Development and Behavior, 6,* 109-158.

Elder, G., Nguyen, T., & Caspi, A. (1985). Linking family hardship to children's lives. *Child Development, 56,* 361-375.

Elliot, D. S., Huizinga, D., & Ageton, S. S. (1985). *Explaining delinquency and drug use.* Beverly Hills, CA: Sage.

Ensminger, M. E., Lamkin, R. P., & Jacobson, N. (1996). School leaving: A longitudinal perspective including neighborhood effects. *Child Development, 67,* 2400-2416.

Entwisle, D. R., & Astone, N. M. (1994). Some practical guidelines for measuring youth's race/ethnicity and socioeconomic status. *Child Development, 65,* 1521-1540.

Entwisle, D. R., Alexander, K. L., & Olson, L. S. (1994). The gender gap in math: Possible origins in neighborhood effects. *American Sociological Review, 59,* 822-838.

Fabrega, H., Ulrich, R., & Loeber, R. (1996). Adolescent psychopathology as a function of informant and risk status. *Journal of Nervous and Mental Disease, 184,* 27-34.

Fantuzzo, J. W., McDermott, P. A., Manz, P. H., Hampton, V. R., & Burdick, N. A. (1996). The Pictorial Scale of Perceived Competence and Social Acceptance: Does it work with low-income urban children? *Child Development, 67,* 10711084.

Farber, E. A., & Egeland, B. (1987). Invulnerability among abused and neglected children. In E. J. Anthony & B. J. Cohler (Eds.), *The invulnerable child* (pp. 253-288). New York: Guilford Press.

Felner, R. D., Aber, M. S., Primavera, J., & Cauce, A. M. (1985). Adaptation and vulnerability in high-risk adolescents: An examination of environmental mediators. *American Journal of Community Psychology, 13,* 365-379.

Felner, R. D., Brand, S., DuBois, D. L., Adan, A. M., Mulhall, P. F., & Evans, E. G. (1995). Socioeconomic disadvantage, proximal environmental experiences, and socio-emotional and academic adjustment in early adolescence: Investigation of a mediated effects model. *Child Development, 66,* 774-792.

Felsman, J. K., & Vaillant, G. E. (1987). Resilient children as adults: A 40 year study. In E. J. Anthony & B. J. Cohler (Eds.), *The invulnerable child* (pp. 289-314). New York: Guilford.

Fergusson, D.M., Horwood, L. J., & Lynskey M. (1994). The childhoods of multiple problem adolescents: A 15-year longitudinal study. *Journal of Child Psychiatry, 35,* 1128-1140.

Fergusson, D. M., & Lynskey, M. T. (1996). Adolescent resiliency to family adversity. *Journal of Child Psychology & Psychiatry, 37,* 281-292.

Finn, J. D., & Rock, D. A. (1997). Academic success among students at risk for school failure. *Journal of Applied Psychology, 82,* 221-234.

Fitzpatrick, K. M. (1993). Exposure to violence and presence of depression among low-income African-American youth. *Journal of Consulting and Clinical Psychology, 61,* 528-531.

Flanagan, C. A. (1990). Change in family work status: Effects on parent-adolescent decision making. *Child Development, 61,* 163-177.

Florsheim, P., Tolan, P. H., & Gorman-Smith, D. (1996). Family process and risk for externalizing behavior problems among African-American and Hispanic boys. *Journal of Consulting and Clinical Psychology, 64,* 1222-1230.

Ford, D. Y., & Harris, J. J., III. (1996). Perceptions and attitudes of Black students toward school, achievement, and other educational variables. *Child Development, 67,* 1141-1152.

Fordham, S., & Ogbu, J. U. (1986). Black students' school success: Coping with the burden of "acting white." *The Urban Review, 18,* 176-206.

Fowler, C. M. (1996). *Before women had wings.* New York: Fawcett Columbine.

Freeman, L. N., Mokros, H., & Poznanzki, E. O. (1993). Violent events reported by normal urban school-aged children: Characteristics and depression correlates. *Journal of the American Academy of Child and Adolescent Psychiatry, 32,* 419-423.

Furstenberg, F. F., Jr., & Harris, K. M. (1993). When and why fathers matter: Impacts of father involvement on children of adolescent mothers. In R. I. Lerman & T. J. Ooms (Eds.), *Young unwed fathers* (pp. 117-138). Philadelphia: Temple University Press.

Garbarino, J. (1995). The American war zone: What children can tell us about living with violence. *Developmental and Behavioral Pediatrics, 16,* 431-434.

Garbarino, J., Kostelny, K., & Dubrow, N. (1991). *No place to be a child.* Lexington, MA: Lexington Books.

Garbarino, J., & Sherman, D. (1980). High-risk neighborhoods and high-risk families: The human ecology of child maltreatment. *Child Development, 51,* 188-198.

Garcia Coll, C., Lamberty, G., Jenkins, R., McAdoo, H. P., Crnic, K., Wasik, B. H., & Vasquez Garcia, H. (1996). An integrative model for the study of developmental competencies in minority children. *Child Development, 67,* 1891-1914.

Garcia Coll, C. T., Meyer, E. C., & Brillon, L. (1995). Ethnic and minority parenting. In M. H. Bornstein (Ed.), *Handbook of parenting* (Vol. 2, pp. 189-210). Mahwah, NJ: Erlbaum.

Garcia Coll, C. T., & Vasquez Garcia, H. A. (1995). Hispanic children and their families: On a different track from the very beginning. In H. E. Fitzgerald, B. M. Lester, & B. Zuckerman (Eds.), *Children of poverty: Research, health, and policy issues* (pp. 57-83). New York: Garland Publishing.

Garmezy, N. (1991). Resiliency and vulnerability to adverse developmental outcomes associated with poverty. *American Behavioral Scientist, 34,* 416-430.

Gaudin, J. M., Polansky, N. A., Kilpatrick, A. C., & Shilton, P. (1993). Loneliness, depression, stress, and social supports in neglectful families. *American Journal of Orthopsychiatry, 63,* 597-605.

Geronimus, A. T. & Korenman, S. (1992). The socioeconomic consequences of teen childbearing reconsidered. *Quarterly Journal of Economics,* November, 1187-1214.

Ginsburg, H. P. (1986). The myth of the deprived child: New thoughts on poor children. In U. Neisser (Ed.), *The school achievement of minority children: New perspectives* (pp. 169-189). Hillsdale, NJ: Erlbaum.

Giovannoni, J., & Billingsley, A. (1970). Child neglect among the poor: A study of parental adequacy in families of three ethnic groups. *Child Welfare,* 196-204.

Glueck, S., & Glueck, E. (1950). *Unraveling juvenile delinquency.* New York: Commonwealth Fund.

Gonzales, N. A., Cauce, A. M., Friedman, R., & Mason, C. A. (In press). Family, peer and neighborhood influences on academic achievement among African-American adolescents: One year prospective effects. *American Journal of Community Psychology.*

Goodman, R., Simonoff, E., & Stevenson, J. (1995). The impact of child IQ, parent IQ, and sibling IQ on child behavioral deviance scores. *Journal of Child Psychology and Psychiatry, 36,* 409-425.

Graham, S. (1992). "Most of the subjects were white and middle class." *American Psychologist, 47,* 629-639.

Graham, S., & Hoehn, S. (1995). Children's understanding of aggression and withdrawal as social stigmas: An attributional analysis. *Child Development, 66,* 1143-1161.

Graham, S., & Hudley, C. (1994). Attributions of aggressive and nonaggressive African-American male early adolescents: A study of construct accessibility. *Developmental Psychology, 30,* 365-373.

Haapasalo, J., & Tremblay, R.E. (1994). Physically aggressive boys from ages 6 to 12: Family background, parenting behavior and prediction of delinquency. *Journal of Consulting and Clinical Psychology, 62,* 1044-105.

Hammond, W. R., & Yung, B. (1993). Psychology's role in the public health response to assaultive violence among young African-American men. *American Psychologist, 48,* 142-154.

Harnish, J. D., Dodge, K. A., & Valente, E. (1995). Mother-child interaction quality as a partial mediator of the roles of maternal depressive symptomatology and socio-economic status in the development of child behavior problems. *Child Development, 66,* 739-753.

Harwood, R. L., Schoelmerich, A., Ventura Cook, E., Schulze, P. A., & Wilson, S. P. (1996). Culture and class influences on Anglo and Puerto Rican mothers' beliefs regarding long-term socialization goals and child behavior. *Child Development, 67,* 2446-2461.

Hashima, P. Y., & Amato, P. R. (1994). Poverty, social support, and parental behavior. *Child Development, 65,* 394-403.

Hauser, R. M. (1994). Measuring socioeconomic status in studies of child development. *Child Development, 65,* 1541-1545.

Hauser, R. M., & Sweeney, M. M. (1997). Does poverty in adolescence affect the life chances of high school graduates? In G. J. Duncan & J. Brooks-Gunn (Eds.), *Consequences of growing up poor* (pp. 518-540). New York: Russell Sage.

Hausman, B., & Hammen, C. (1993). Parenting in homeless families: The double crisis. *American Journal of Orthopsychiatry, 63,* 358-369.

Hawley, T. L., & Disney, E. R. (1992). Crack's children: The consequences of maternal cocaine abuse. *Society for Research in Child Development Social Policy Report, 6,* (Winter).

Hawkins, J. D., & Weis, J. G. (1985). The social development model: An integrated approach to delinquency prevention. *Journal of Primary Prevention, 6,* 73-97.

Haynes, N. M., & Comer, J. P. (1996). Integrating schools, families, and communities through successful school reform: The School Development program. *School Psychology Review, 25,* 501-506.

Herrnstein, R. A., & Murray, C. (1994). *The bell curve.* New York: Grove Press.

Hetherington, M. E. (1997). Teenaged childbearing and divorce. In S. S. Luthar, J. A. Burack, D. Cicchetti, & J. R. Weisz, (Eds.), *Developmental psychopathology: Perspectives on adjustment, risk, and disorder* (pp. 350-373). New York: Cambridge.

Hobfoll, S. E., Ritter, C., Lavin, J., Hulsizer, M. R., & Cameron, R. P. (1995). Depression prevalence and incidence among inner-city pregnant and postpartum women. *Journal of Consulting and Clinical Psychology, 63,* 445-453.

Hook, M. P. V. (1990). The Iowa farm crisis: Perceptions, interpretations, and family patterns. In V. C. McLoyd & C. A. Flanagan (Eds.), *New Directions for Child Development* (Vol 46, pp. 71-86). San Francisco: Jossey Bass.

Hubbs-Tait, L., Hughes, K. P., Culp, A. M., Osofsky, J. D., Hann, D. M., Eberhart-Wright, A., & Ware, L. M. (1996). Children of adolescent mothers: Attachment representation, maternal depression, and later behavior problems. *American Journal of Orthopsychiatry, 66,* 416426.

Huston, A. C. (1994a). Children in poverty: Developmental and policy issues. In A. C. Huston (Ed.), *Children in poverty* (pp. 1-22). New York: Cambridge.

Huston, A. C. (1994b). Children in poverty: Designing research to affect policy. *Social Policy Report, 8,* 1-12. Ann Arbor, MI: Society for Research in Child Development.

Huston, A. C., McLoyd, V. C., & Garcia Coll, C. (1994). Children and poverty: Issues in contemporary research. *Child Development, 65,* 275-282.

Huston, A. C., McLoyd, V. C., & Garcia Coll, C. (1998). Poverty and behavior: The case for multiple methods and levels of analysis. *Developmental Review, 17,* 376-393.

Jarrett, R. L. (1990). *A comparative examination of socialization patterns among low-income African-Americans, Chicanos, Puerto Ricans, and whites: A review of the ethnographic literature.* Washington, DC: Social Sciences Research Council.

Jarrett, R. L. (1994). Living poor: Family life among single parent, African-American women. *Social Problems, 41,* 30-49.

Jarrett, R. L. (1995). Growing up poor: The family experiences of socially mobile youth in low-income African-American neighborhoods. *Journal of Adolescent Research, 10,* 111-135.

Jessor, R., Van Den Bos, J., Vanderryn, J., Costa, F. M., & Turbin, M. S. (1995). Protective factors in adolescent problem behavior: Moderator effects and developmental change. *Developmental Psychology, 31,* 923-933.

Juarez, S. C., Viega, B., & Richards, M. H. (1997, April). *The moderating effect of family environment on exposure to violence and PTSD symptoms.* Paper presented at the biennial conference of the Society for Research on Child Development, Washington DC.

Kagan, J. (1971). *Change and continuity in infancy.* New York: Wiley.

Kazdin, A. E. (1995). *Conduct disorders in childhood and adolescence* (2nd ed). Thousand Oaks, CA: Sage.

Kellam, S. G. (1987). Contributions by the Society for Life History Research on psychopathology: Epidemiology, life course development, and family research. *Psychiatry, 50,* 303-307.

Kellam, S. G., Ensminger, M. E., & Turner, R. J. (1977). Family structure and the mental health of children: Concurrent and longitudinal community wide studies. *Archives of General Psychiatry, 34,* 1012-1022.

Kelley, M. L., Power, T. G., Wimbush, D. D. (1992). Determinants of disciplinary practices in low-income black mothers. *Child Development, 63,* 573-582.

Kendler, K. (1995). Genetic epidemiology in psychiatry: Taking both genes and environment seriously. *Archives of General Psychiatry, 52,* 895-899.

Kessler, R. C., McGonagle, K. A., Zhao, S., Nelson, C. B., Hughes, M., Eshleman, S., Wittchen, H., & Kendler, K. S. (1994). Lifetime and 12-month prevalence of DSM-IIIR psychiatric disorders in the United States. *Archives of General Psychiatry, 51,* 8-19.

Kessler, R. C., & Neighbors, H. W. (1986). A new perspective on the relationships among race, social class, and psychological distress. *Journal of Health and Social Behavior, 27,* 107-115.

Klerman, L. V. (1994). The health of poor children: Problems and programs. In A. C. Huston (Ed.), *Children in poverty* (pp. 136-157). New York: Cambridge.

Knitzer, J. (1996). Children's mental health: Changing programs and policies. In E. F. Zigler, S. L. Kagan, & N. W. Hall (Eds.), *Children, families, and government: Preparing for the 21st century* (pp. 207-232). New York: Cambridge.

Knitzer, J. (In press). Early childhood mental health services through a policy and systems perspective. In S. J. Meisels & J. P. Shonkoff, (Eds.), *Handbook of early childhood intervention* (2nd ed.). New York: Cambridge.

Koblinsky, S. A., Morgan, K. M., & Anderson, E. A. (1997). African-American homeless and low-income housed mothers: Comparison of parenting practices. *American Journal of Orthopsychiatry, 67.* 37-47.

Kupersmidt, J. B., Griesler, P. C., DeRosier, M. E., Patterson, C. J., & Davis, P. W. (1995). Childhood aggression and peer relations in the context of family and neighborhood factors. *Child Development, 66,* 360375.

Leadbeater, B. J., Bishop, S. J., & Raver, C. C. (1996). Quality of mother-toddler interactions, maternal depressive symptoms, and behavior problems in preschoolers of adolescent mothers. *Developmental Psychology, 32,* 280-288.

Leadbeater, B. J., Hellner, I., Allen, P. J., Aber, J. L. (1989). Assessment of interpersonal negotiation strategies in youth engaged in problem behaviors. *Developmental Psychology, 25,* 465-472

Leadbeater, B. J., Way, N., & Raden, A. (1997). Why not marry your baby's father? Answers from African-American and Hispanic adolescent mothers. In B. J. Leadbeater & N. Way (Eds.), *Urban girls: Resisting stereotypes, creating identities* (pp. 193-212). New York: New York University Press.

LeCompte, M. D., & Preissle, J. (1993). *Ethnography and qualitative design in educational research.* New York: Academic Press.

Lempers, J. D., Clark-Lempers, D., & Simons, R. L. (1989). Economic hardship, parenting, and distress in adolescence. *Child Development, 60,* 25-39.

Lepper, M. R., Sethi, S., Dialdin, D., & Drake, M. (1997). Intrinsic and extrinsic motivation: A developmental perspective. In S. S. Luthar, J. Burack, D. Cicchetti, and J. Weisz (Eds.), *Developmental psychopathology: Perspectives on adjustment, risk, and disorder* (pp. 23-50). New York: Cambridge.

Lerman, R. L., & Ooms, T. J. (1993). *Young unwed fathers.* Philadelphia: Temple University Press.

Lewis, O. (1966). The culture of poverty. *Scientific American, 215,* 19-25.

Lipman, E. L., & Offord, D. R. (1997). Psychosocial morbidity among poor children in Ontario. In G. J. Duncan & J. Brooks-Gunn (Eds.), *Consequences of growing up poor* (pp. 239-287). New York: Russell Sage.

Loeber, R., & Dishion, T. (1983). Early predictors of male delinquency: A review. *Psychological Bulletin, 94,* 68-99.

Luster, T., & McAdoo, H. P. (1994). Factors related to the achievement and adjustment of young African American children. *Child Development, 65,* 1080-1094.

Luster, T., & McAdoo, H. (1996). Family and child influences on educational attainment: A secondary analysis of the High/Scope Perry Preschool data. *Developmental Psychology, 32(1),,* 26-39.

Luthar, S. S. (1991). Vulnerability and resilience: A study of high-risk adolescents. *Child Development, 62,* 600-616.

Luthar, S. S. (1995). Social competence in the school setting: Prospective cross-domain associations among inner-city teens. *Child Development, 66,* 416-429.

Luthar, S. S. (1997). Sociodemographic disadvantage and psychosocial adjustment: Perspectives from developmental psychopathology. In S. S. Luthar, J. A. Burack, D. Cicchetti, & J. R. Weisz, (Eds.), *Developmental Psychopathology: Perspectives on adjustment, risk, and disorder* (pp. 459-485). New York: Cambridge.

Luthar, S. S., & Burack, J. A. (in press). Adolescent wellness: In the eye of the beholder? In D. Cicchetti, J. Rappaport, I. Sandler, & R. Weissberg (Eds.), *The promotion of wellness in children and adolescents.* Thousand Oaks, CA: Sage.

Luthar, S. S., & Cushing, G. (1997). Substance use and personal adjustment among disadvantaged teenagers: A six-month prospective study. *Journal of Youth and Adolescence, 26,* 353-372.

Luthar, S. S., Cushing, G., & McMahon, T. (1997). Substance abusers and their families: Developmental perspectives. In S. S. Luthar, J. Burack, D. Cicchetti, and J. Weisz (Eds.), *Developmental psychopathology: Perspectives on adjustment, risk, and disorder* (pp. 437-458). New York: Cambridge.

Luthar, S. S., Cushing, G., Merikangas, K., & Rounsaville, B. J. (1998). Multiple jeopardy: Risk/protective factors among addicted mothers' offspring. *Development & Psychopathology, 10,* 117-136.

Luthar, S. S., & McMahon, T. (1996). Peer reputation among adolescents: Use of the Revised Class Play with inner-city teens. *Journal of Research on Adolescence, 6,* 581-603.

Luthar, S. S., & Suchman, N. E. (In press). Relational psychotherapy mothers' group: A developmentally informed intervention for at-risk mothers. *Development & Psychopathology.* Rochester, NY: University of Rochester Press.

Luthar, S. S., & Zigler, E. (1991). Vulnerability and competence: A review of research on resilience in childhood. *American Journal of Orthopsychiatry, 61,* 6-22.

Lyons-Ruth, K., Zoll, D., Connell, D., Grunebaum, H. U. (1989). Family deviance and family disruption in childhood: Association with maternal behavior and infant maltreatment during the first two years of life. *Development & Psychopathology, 1,* 219-236.

Lynam, D., Moffitt, T., & Stouthamer-Loeber, M. (1993). Explaining the relation between IQ and delinquency: Class, race, test motivation, school failure, or self-control? *Journal of Abnormal Psychology, 102,* 187-196.

MacPhee, D., Fritz, J., & Miller-Heyl, J. (1996). Ethnic variations in personal social networks and parenting. *Child Development, 67,* 3278-3295.

MacPhee, D., Kreutzer, J. C., & Fritz, J. J. (1994). Infusing a diversity perspective into human development courses. *Child Development, 65,* 699-715.

Magnusson, D., & Bergman, L. (1988). Individual and variable-based approaches to longitudinal research on early risk factors. In M. Rutter (Ed.), *Studies of Psychosocial Risk* (pp. 45-61). Cambridge, Great Britain: Cambridge.

Marans, S.,& Adelman, A. (1997). Experiencing violence in a developmental context. In J. D. Osofsky (Ed.), *Children in a violent society* (pp. 202-221). New York: Guilford.

Marans, S., Adnopoz, J., Berkman, M., Esserman, D., MacDonald, D., Nagler, S., Randall, R., Schaefer, M., & Wearing, M. (1995). *Police mental health partnership: A community based response to urban violence.* New Haven, CT: Yale University Press.

Martinez, P., & Richters, J. E. (1993). The NIMH Community Violence Project: II. Children's distress symptoms associated with violence exposure. *Psychiatry, 56,* 22-35.

Mason, C. A., Cauce, A. M., Gonzales, N., & Hiraga, Y. (1996). Neither too sweet nor too sour: Problem peers, maternal control, and problem behavior in African American adolescents. *Child Development, 67,* 2115-2130.

Mason, C. A., Cauce, A. M., Gonzales, N., Hiraga, Y., & Grove, K. (1994). An ecological model of externalizing behaviors in African-American adolescents: No family is an island. *Journal of Research on Adolescence, 4,* 639-655.

Masten, A. S., Best, K. M., & Garmezy, N. (1990). Resilience and development: Contributions from the study of children who overcome adversity. *Development & Psychopathology, 2,* 425-444.

Masten, A. S., Sesma, A., Si-Asar, R., Lawrence, C., Miliotis, D., & Dionne, J. A. (1997). Educational risks for children experiencing homelessness. *Journal of School Psychology, 35,* 27-46.

Mayer, S. E. (1997). *What money can't buy: Family income and children's life chances.* Cambridge, MA: Harvard University Press.

Mayes, L. C., & Bornstein, M. H. (1997). The development of children exposed to cocaine. In S. S. Luthar, J. Burack, D. Cicchetti, & J. R. Weisz (Eds.), *Developmental psychopathology: Perspectives on adjustment, risk, and disorder* (pp. 166-188). New York: Cambridge.

McGee R., Feehan M., Williams, S., & Anderson, J. (1992). DSM-III disorders from age 11 to age 15 years. *Journal of the American Academy of Child and Adolescent Psychiatry, 31,* 50-59.

McGee, R. A., Wolfe, D. A., & Wilson, S. K. (1997). Multiple maltreatment experiences and adolescent behavior problems: Adolescents' perspectives. *Development & Psychopathology, 9,* 131-150.

McLanahan, S., & Sandefur, G. (1994). *Growing up with a single parent: What hurts, what helps.* Cambridge, MA: Harvard University Press.

McLanahan, S. S. (1997). Parent absence or poverty: Which matters more? In G. J. Duncan & J. Brooks-Gunn (Eds.), *Consequences of growing up poor* (pp. 35–48). New York: Russell Sage.

McLoyd, V. C. (1990). The impact of economic hardship on Black families and children: Psychological distress, parenting, and socioemotional development. *Child Development, 61,* 311-346.

McLoyd, V. C. (1997). Children in poverty: Development, public policy, and practice. In W. Damon, I. E. Siegel, & K. A. Renninger (Eds.), *Handbook of child psychology (5th ed.): Child psychology in practice* (pp. 135-208). New York: Wiley.

McLoyd, V. C., Jayaratne, T. E., Ceballo, R., & Borquez, J. (1994). Unemployment and work interruption among African-American single mothers: Effects on parenting and adolescent socioemotional functioning. *Child Development, 65,* 562-589.

McLoyd, V. C., & Wilson, L. (1990). Maternal behavior, social support, and economic conditions as predictors of distress in children. In V. C. McLoyd & C. A. Flanagan (Eds.), *New directions for child development (Vol. 46) Economic stress: Effects on family life and child development.* San Francisco: Jossey-Bass

McLoyd, V. C., & Wilson, L. (1994). The strain of living poor: Parenting, social support, and child mental health. In A. C. Huston (Ed.), *Children in poverty* (pp. 105-135). New York: Cambridge.

108   POVERTY AND CHILDREN'S ADJUSTMENT

Merton, R. K. (1968). *Social theory and social structure* (enlarged ed.). New York: Free Press.
Miringoff, M. L., Miringoff, M., & Opdycke, S. (1996). Monitoring the nation's social performance: The index of social health. In E. F. Zigler, S. L. Kagan, & N. W. Hall (Eds.), *Children, families, and government: Preparing for the 21st century* (pp. 10-30). New York: Cambridge.
Moffitt, T. E. (1993a). Adolescence-limited and life-course-persistent antisocial behavior: A developmental taxonomy. *Psychological Review, 100,* 674-701.
Moffitt, T. E. (1993b). Neuropsychology of conduct disorder. *Development & Psychopathology, 5,* 135-151.
Mowry, J. (1992). *Way past cool.* New York: Harper Perennial.
Murphy, J. M., Jellinek, M., Quinn, D., Smith, G., Poitrast, F. G., & Goshko, M. (1991). Substance abuse and serious child mistreatment: Prevalence, risk, and outcome in a court sample. *Child Abuse and Neglect, 15,* 197-211.
National Adolescent Health Resource Center (1996). *Voice of Connecticut Youth: A statewide survey of adolescent health.* Minneapolis, MN: University of Minnesota.
National Center for Children in Poverty (1996). *One in four: America's youngest poor.* New York: Columbia School of Public Health.
National Research Council. (1993). *Losing generations: Adolescents in high-risk settings.* Washington, DC: National Academy Press.
Natriello, G., McDill, E. L., & Pallas, A. M. (1990). *Schooling disadvantaged children: Racing against catastrophe.* New York: Teachers College Press
Neighbors, H. W., & Jackson, J. S. (Eds.) (1996). *Mental health in black America.* Thousand Oaks, CA: Sage.
Nitz, K., Ketterlinus, R. D., & Brandt, L. J. (1995). The role of stress, social support, and family environment in adolescent mothers' parenting. *Journal of Adolescent Research, 10,* 358-382.
O'Connor, T. G., & Rutter, M. (1996). Risk mechanisms in development: Some conceptual and methodological considerations. *Developmental Psychology, 32,* 787-795.
Offord, D., Boyle, M., & Racine, Y. (1991). *Ontario child health study: Children at risk.* Ontario, Canada: Queen's Printer for Ontario.
Ogbu, J. U. (1988). A cultural ecology of competence among inner-city blacks. In M. Spencer, G. Brookins, & W. Allen (Eds.), *Beginnings: The social and affective development of black children* (pp. 45-66). Hillsdale, NJ: Erlbaum.
Ogbu, J. U. (1991). Minority coping responses and school experience. *Journal of Psychohistory, 18,* 433-456.
Osborn, A. F. (1990). Resilient children: A longitudinal study of high achieving socially disadvantaged children. *Early Child Development and Care, 62,* 23-47.
Osofsky, J. D. (1995). The effects of exposure to violence on young children. *American Psychologist, 50,* 782-788.
Peterson, P. L., Hawkins, J. D., Abbott, R. D., & Catalano, R. F. (1994). Disentangling the effects of parental drinking, family management, and parental alcohol norms on current drinking by black and white adolescents. *Journal of Research on Adolescence, 4,* 203-227.
Phinney, J. S. (1990). Ethnic identity in adolescents and adults: Review of research. *Psychological Bulletin, 108,* 499-514.

Pianta, R. & Egeland, B. (1990). Life stress and parenting outcomes in a disadvantaged sample: Results of the Mother-Child Interaction project. *Journal of Clinical Child Psychology, 19,* 329-336.

Pianta, R. C., & Egeland, B. (1994). Relation between depressive symptoms and stressful life events in a sample of disadvantaged mothers. *Journal of Consulting and Clinical Psychology, 62,* 1229-1234.

Pianta, R. C., Egeland, B. & Sroufe, L. A. (1990). Maternal stress and children's development: prediction of school outcomes and identification of protective factors. In J. Rolf, A. S. Masten, D. Cicchetti, K. H. Nuechterlein, & S. Weintraub (Eds.), *Risk and protective factors in the development of psychopathology* (pp. 215-235). New York: Cambridge.

Plomin, R. D. (1994). *Genetics and experience: The interplay between nature and nurture.* Thousand Oaks, CA: Sage.

Plomin, R. (1995). Genetics and children's experiences in the family. *Journal of Child Psychology and Psychiatry, 36,* 33-68.

Posner, J. K., & Vandell, D. L. (1994). Low-income children's after-school care: Are there beneficial effects of after-school programs? *Child Development, 65,* 440-456.

Prinz, R. J., & Miller, G. E. (1991). Issues in understanding and treating childhood conduct problems in disadvantaged populations. *Journal of Clinical Child Psychology, 20,* 379-385.

Quay, H. C. (1993). The psychobiology of undersocialized aggressive conduct disorder: A theoretical perspective. *Development & Psychopathology, 5,* 165-180.

Quinton, D., Rutter, M., & Gulliver, L. (1990). Continuities in psychiatric disorders from childhood to adulthood in the children of psychiatric patients. In L. Robins & M. Rutter (Eds.), *Straight and devious pathways from childhood to adulthood* (pp. 259-278). New York: Cambridge.

Rende, R., & Plomin, R. (1993). Families at risk for psychopathology: Who becomes affected and why? *Development & Psychopathology, 5,* 529-540.

Reis, J., Barbera-Stein, L., & Bennett, S. (1986). Ecological determinants of parenting. *Family Relations, 35,* 547-554.

Reynolds, A. J. (1998). Resilience among black urban youth: Prevalence, intervention effects, and mechanisms of influence. *American Journal of Orthopsychiatry, 68,* 84-100.

Richters, J. E., & Cicchetti, D. (1993). Mark Twain meets DSM-IIIR: Conduct disorders, development, and the concept of harmful dysfunction. *Development & Psychopathology, 5,* 5-29.

Richters, J. E., & Martinez, P. E. (1993). Violent communities, family choices, and children's chances: An algorithm for improving the odds. *Development & Psychopathology, 5,* 609-627.

Ripple, C., & Luthar, S. S. (1998). *Long-term predictors of academic adjustment and high school dropout among inner-city adolescents.* Manuscript submitted for publication.

Rogler, L. H. (1996). Editorial: Increasing socioeconomic inequalities and the mental health of the poor. *Journal of Nervous and Mental Disease, 184,* 719-722.

Rowe, D. C., & Rodgers, J. L. (1998). Poverty and behavior: Are environmental measures nature and nurture? *Developmental Review, 17,* 358-375.

Rowe, D. C., Vazsonyi, A. T., Flannery, D. J. (1994). No more than skin deep: Ethnic and racial similarity in developmental process. *Psychological Review, 101,* 396-413.
Rutter, M. (1979). Protective factors in children's responses to stress and disadvantage. In M. W. Kent, & J. E. Rolf (Eds.), *Primary prevention in psychopathology* (pp. 49-74). Hanover, NH: University Press of New England.
Rutter, M. (1989a). Temperament: Conceptual issues and clinical implications. In G. A. Kohnstamm, J. E. Bates, & M. K. Rothbart (Eds.), *Temperament in childhood* (pp. 463-479). New York: Wiley.
Rutter, M. (1989b). Isle of Wight revisited: Twenty-five years of child psychiatric epidemiology. *Journal of the American Academy of Child and Adolescent Psychiatry, 28,* 633-653.
Rutter, M. (1990). Psychosocial resilience and protective mechanisms. In J. Rolf, A. S. Masten, D. Cicchetti, K. H. Nuechterlein, & S. Weintraub (Eds.), *Risk and protective factors in the development of psychopathology* (pp. 181-214). New York: Cambridge.
Sameroff, A. J., & Chandler, M. J. (1975). Reproductive risk and the continuum of caretaking casualty. In F. D. Horowitz, M. Hetherington, S. Scarr-Salapatek, & G. Siegel (Eds.), *Review of child development research* (Vol. 43, pp. 187-244). Chicago: University of Chicago.
Sameroff, A. J., Seifer, R., Zax, M., & Barocas, R. (1987). Early indicators of developmental risk: The Rochester Longitudinal Study. *Schizophrenia Bulletin, 13,* 383-393.
Sameroff, A. J., Seifer, R., & Bartko, W. T. (1997). Environmental perspectives on adaptation during childhood and adolescence. In S. S. Luthar, J. A. Burack, D. Cicchetti, & J. R. Weisz, (Eds.), *Developmental Psychopathology: Perspectives on adjustment, risk, and disorder* (pp. 507-526). New York: Cambridge.
Sampson, R. J., & Laub, J. H. (1994). Urban poverty and the family context of delinquency: A new look at structure and process in a classic study. *Child Development, 65,* 523-540.
Sampson, R. J., Raudenbush, S. W., & Earls, F. (1997). Neighborhoods and violent crime: A multilevel study of collective efficacy. *Science, 277,* 918-924.
Sanders-Phillips, K., Moisan, P. A., Wadlington, S., Morgan, S., English, K.(1995). Ethnic difference in psychological functioning among black and latino sexually abused girls. *Child Abuse & Neglect, 19,* 691-706.
Schnitzer, P. K. (1996). "They don't come in!" Stories told, lessons taught about poor families in therapy. *American Journal of Orthopsychiatry, 66,* 572-582.
Schwab-Stone, M. E., Ayers, T. S., Kasprow, W., Voyce, C., Barone, C., Shriver, T., Weissberg, R. P. (1995). No safe haven: A study of violence exposure in an urban community. *Journal of the American Academy of Child and Adolescent Psychiatry, 34,* 1343-1352.
Schweinhart, L. J., Barnes, H. V., & Weikart, D. P. (Eds.) (1993). *Significant benefits: The High/Scope Perry Preschool Study through age 27.* Ypsilanti, MI: High/Scope.
Seidman, E., Allen, L., Aber, J. L., Mitchell, C., & Feinman, J. (1994). The impact of school transitions in early adolescence on the self-system and perceived social context of poor urban youth. *Child Development, 65,* 507-522.
Seitz, V. (In press). Effective interventions for adolescent mothers. *Clinical Psychology: Science and Practice.*

Seitz, V., & Apfel, N. H. (1997, April). *Gender of the firstborn child affects life outcomes for urban teenage mothers.* Poster presented at the biennial conference of the Society for Research on Child Development, Washington DC.

Shaw, D. S., Owens, E. B., Vondra, J. I., & Keenan, K., & Winslow, E. B. (1996). Early risk factors and pathways in the development of early disruptive behavior problems. *Development & Psychopathology, 8,* 679-699.

Shaw, D. S., Vondra, J. I., Hommerding, K. D., Keenan, K., & Dunn, M. (1994). Chronic family adversity and early child behavior problems: A longitudinal study of low income families. *Journal of Child Psychology and Psychiatry, 35,* 1109-1122.

Simon, D., & Burns, E. (1997). *The corner: A year in the life of an inner-city neighborhood.* New York: Broadway Books.

Singer, M. I., Anglin, T. M., Song, L. Y., & Lunghofer, L. (1995). Adolescents' exposure to violence and associated symptoms of psychological trauma. *Journal of the American Medical Association, 273,* 477-482.

Slaughter-Defoe, D. T., Nakagawa, K., Takanishi, R., & Johnson, D. J. (1990). Toward cultural/ecological perspectives on schooling and achievement in African- and Asian-American children. *Child Development, 61,* 363-383.

Smith, J., & Prior, M. (1995). Temperament and stress resilience in school-age children: A within-families study. *Journal of the American Academy of Child & Adolescent Psychiatry, 34,* 168-179.

Sontag, D. (1997, August 11). U.S. deports felons but can't keep them out. *New York Times,* p. A8.

Spencer, M.B. (1988). Self-concept development. In D. T. Slaughter (Ed.), Black children and poverty: A developmental perspective. *New Directions for Child Development 42,* pp. 59-72. San Francisco: Jossey-Bass.

Spencer, M. B. (1995). Old issues and new theorizing about African-American Youth: A phenomenological variant of ecological systems theory. In R. L. Taylor (Ed.), *Black youth: Perspectives on their status in the United States* (pp. 37-69). Westport, CT: Praeger.

Spencer, M. B., Cole, S. P., DuPree, D., Glymph, A., & Pierre, P. (1993). Self-efficacy among urban African American early adolescents: Exploring issues of risk, vulnerability, and resilience. *Development & Psychopathology, 5,* 719-739.

Spencer M. B., & Markstom-Adams, C. (1990). Identity processes among racial and ethnic minority children in America. *Child Development, 61,* 290-310.

Sroufe, L. A., Egeland, B., & Kreutzer, T. (1990). The fate of early experience following developmental change: Longitudinal approaches to individual adaptation in childhood. *Child Development, 61,* 1363-1373.

Sroufe, L. A., & Rutter, M. (1984). The domain of developmental psychopathology. *Child Development, 55,* 17-29.

Stattin, H., & Magnusson, D. (1996). Antisocial development: A holistic approach. *Development & Psychopathology, 8,* 617-646.

Steinberg, L. (1987, April 25). Why Japan's students outdo ours. *New York Times,* p. A15.

Steinberg, L. L., Darling, N. E., Fletcher, A. C., Brown, B. B, & Dornbusch, S. M. (1995). Authoritative parenting and adolescent adjustment: An ecological journey. In P. Moen, G. H. Elder, & K. Luscher (Eds.), *Examining lives in context: Perspectives on the ecology of human development* (pp. 423-466). Washington, DC: American Psychological Association.

Steele, C. M. (1997). A threat in the air: How stereotypes shape intellectual identity and performance. *American Psychologist, 52,* 613-629.

Stevens, J. H. (1988). Social support, locus of control, and parenting in three low-income groups of mothers: black teenagers, black adults, and white adults. *Child Development, 59,* 635-642.

Stipek, D. (1997). Success in school: for a head start in life. In S. S. Luthar, J. Burack, D. Cicchetti, and J. Weisz (Eds.), *Developmental psychopathology: Perspectives on adjustment, risk, and disorder* (pp. 75-92). New York: Cambridge.

Sullivan, M. L. (1996). Developmental transitions in poor youth: Delinquency and crime. In J. A. Graber, J. Brooks-Gunn, and A. C. Petersen (Eds.), *Transitions through adolescence: Interpersonal domains and context* (pp. 141-164). Mahwah, NJ: Erlbaum.

Tarter, R. E., & Vanyukov, M. (in press). Re-visiting the validity of the construct of resilience. In M. Glantz, Z. Sloboda, and L. C. Huffman, (Eds.), *Resiliency and development: Positive life adaptations.* New York: Plenum.

Taylor, R. D. (1996). Adolescents' perceptions of kinship support and family management practices: Associations with adolescent adjustment in African-American families. *Developmental Psychology, 32,* 687-695.

Taylor, R. D., Casten, R., & Flickinger, S. (1993). The influence of kinship social support on the parenting experiences and psychosocial adjustment of African American adolescents. *Developmental Psychology, 29,* 382-388.

Tolan, P. T. (1996). How resilient is the concept of resilience? *The Community Psychologist, 29,* 12-15.

Trickett, P. K., Aber, J. L., Carlson, V., & Cicchetti, D. (1991). Relationship of socioeconomic status to the etiology and developmental sequelae of physical child abuse. *Developmental Psychology, 27,* 148-158

Verhulst, F. C., & Koot, H. M. (1992). *Child psychiatric epidemiology: Concepts, methods, and findings.* Newbury Park, CA: Sage.

Wakschlag, L. S., Chase-Lansdale, P. L., Brooks-Gunn, J. (1996). Not just "Ghost in the nursery": Contemporaneous intergenerational relationships and parenting in young African-American families. *Child Development, 67,* 2131-2147.

Wall, J. E., & Holden, E. W. (1994). Aggressive, assertive, and submissive behaviors in disadvantaged, inner-city preschool children. *Journal of Clinical Child Psychology, 23,* 382-390.

Wasserman, G. A., Rauh, V. A., Brunelli, S. A., Garcia-Castro, M., & Necos, B. (1990). Psychosocial attributes and life experiences of disadvantaged minority mothers: age and ethnic variations. *Child Development, 61,* 566-580.

Weist, M. D., Freedman, A. H., Paskewitz, D. A., Proescher, E. J., & Flaherty, L. T. (1995). Urban youth under stress: Empirical identification of protective factors. *Journal of Youth and Adolescence, 24,* 705-721.

Weisz, J., McCarty, C. A., Eastman, K. L., Chaiyasit, W., & Suwanlert, S. (1997). Developmental psychopathology and culture: Ten lessons from Thailand. In S. S. Luthar, J. Burack, D. Cicchetti, and J. Weisz (Eds.), *Developmental psychopathology: Perspectives on adjustment, risk, and disorder* (pp. 568-592). New York: Cambridge.

Wentzel, K. R., & Asher, S. R. (1995). The academic lives of neglected, rejected, popular, and controversial children. *Child Development, 66,* 754-763.

Werner, E. E., & Smith, R. S. (1992). *Overcoming the odds: High risk children from birth to adulthood.* Ithaca, NY: Cornell University Press.

Wilens, T. E., Biederman, J., Kiely, K., Bredin, E., & Spencer, T. J. (1995). Pilot study of behavioral and emotional disturbances in the high-risk children of parents with opioid dependence. *Journal of the American Academy of Child and Adolescent Psychiatry, 34,* 779-785.

Wills, T., Vaccaro, D., & McNamara, G. (1992). The role of life events, family support, and competence in adolescent substance use: A test of vulnerability and protective factors. *American Journal of Community Psychology, 20,* 349-374.

Wilson, M. N. (1984). Mothers' and grandmothers' perceptions of parental behavior in three-generational black families. *Child Development, 55,* 1333-1339.

Wilson, W. J. (1987). *The truly disadvantaged: The inner-city, the underclass, and public policy.* Chicago: The University of Chicago Press.

Wilson, W. J. (1991). Studying inner-city social dislocations: The challenge of public agenda research. *American Sociological Review, 56,* 1-14.

Wyman, P. A., Cowen, E. L., Work, W. C., & Kerley, J. H. (1993). The role of children's future expectations in self-system functioning and adjustment to life-stress: A prospective study of urban at risk children. *Development & Psychopathology, 5,* 649-661.

Wyman, P. A., Cowen, E. L., Work, W. C., & Parker, G. R. (1991). Developmental and family milieu interview correlates of resilience in urban children who have experienced major life-stress. *American Journal of Community Psychology, 19,* 405-426.

Yoshikawa, H. (1994). Prevention as cumulative protection: Effects of early family support and education on chronic delinquency and its risks. *Psychological Bulletin, 115,* 28-54.

Yoshikawa, H., & Knitzer, J. (1997). *Lessons from the field: Head Start mental health strategies to meet changing needs.* New York: National Center for Children in Poverty.

Zaslow, M. J., & Takanishi, R. (1993). Priorities for research in adolescent development. *American Psychologist, 48,* 185-192.

Zigler, E. (1993). Communicating effectively before members of congress. In K. McCartney & D. Phillips (Eds.), *An insider's guide to providing expert testimony before Congress* (pp. 11-15). Chicago: Society for Research in Child Development.

Zigler, E. F., & Gilman, E. (1996). Not just any care: Shaping a coherent child care policy. In E. F. Zigler, S. L. Kagan, & N. W. Hall (Eds.), *Children, families, and government: Preparing for the 21st century* (pp. 94-116). New York: Cambridge.

Zigler, E. F., Kagan, S. L., & Hall, N. W. (Eds.). (1996). *Children, families, and government: Preparing for the 21st century.* New York: Cambridge.

Zigler, E. F., & Styfco, S. (1996). Head Start and early childhood intervention: The changing course of social science and social policy. In E. F. Zigler, S. L. Kagan, & N. W. Hall (Eds.), *Children, families, and government: Preparing for the 21st century* (pp. 132-155). New York: Cambridge.

Zima, B. T., Wells, K. B., Benjamin, B., Duan, N. (1996). Mental health problems among homeless mothers: Relationship to service use and child mental health problems. *Archives of General Psychiatry, 53,* 332-338.

Zimmerman, M. A., Salem, D. A., & Maton, K. I. (1995). Family structure and psychosocial correlates among urban African-American adolescent males. *Child Development, 66,* 1598-1613.

Zuckerman, B. (1994). Effects on parents and children. In D. J. Besharov (Ed.), *When drug addicts have children: Reorienting child welfare's response* (pp. 49-64). Washington, DC: Child Welfare League of America.

AUTHOR INDEX

115

Brunelli, S. A., 25
Brunswick, A., 20
Bryant, D. M., 27
Burack, J. A., 65, 80
Burchinal, M. R., 27, 60
Burgos, W., 68
Burns, B. J., 35
Burns, E., 47, 78
Burton, L., 25, 28, 77, 78, 79

Cadenhead, C., 50
Cameron, R. P., 41
Canino, I., 33
Cantwell, D., 82
Carlson, E., 2
Carlson, V., 49
Caspi, A., 8
Casten, R., 60
Catalano, R. F., 35
Cauce, A. M., 29, 47, 48, 63, 64
Ceballo, R., 8
Chaffin, M., 43, 50
Chaiyasit, W., 3
Chandler, M. J., 75
Chase-Lansdale, P. L., 10, 25, 27, 28, 32,
     44, 68
Chasnoff, I. J., 43
Chavez, E. L., 31
Chow, J., 69
Christoffel, K. K., 34
Chute, C., 40
Cicchetti, D., 16, 18, 41, 49, 50, 51, 64, 71,
     75, 78
Clark-Lempers, D., 13
Clifford, E., 9
Cohler, B. J., 3, 78, 79, 92
Coie, J. D., 63, 64, 65, 71
Cole, R. E., 47
Cole, S. P., 16
Comer, J. P., 62, 89, 90
Conger, K. J., 9
Conger, R. D., 9, 51, 53
Connell, D., 44
Connell, J. P., 9, 11, 16, 19, 27, 48
Costa, F. M., 8
Costello, E. J., 2, 35, 84
Coulton, C. J., 69

Cowen, E. L., 14, 16, 17, 44, 48, 52, 75, 87
Crichlow, W., 9
Crittenden, P. M., 15, 50
Crosby, L., 64
Cross, C. E., 15
Crum, R. M., 43
Cummings, E. M., 41
Cushing, G., 20, 27, 36

Danziger, S., 4
Darling, N. E., 83
Davies, P. T., 41
Davis, P. W., 68
de Vries, M. W., 15
deCubas, M. M., 43
Dembo, R., 68
Denner, J., 46
DeRosier, M. E., 68
Dialdin, D., 62
DiBiase, R., 67
Dishion, T., 64, 83
Disney, E. R., 43
Dodge, K. A., 8, 13, 35, 51, 52, 63, 72
Dornbusch, S. M., 83
Drake, M., 62
Duan, N., 66
DuBois, D. L., 8, 46, 48, 62
Dubow, E. F., 64
Dubrow, N., 71
Dumas, J. E., 42
Duncan, G. J., 12, 13, 23(n4), 30, 68, 83
Dunn, L. M., 45
Dunn, M., 8
DuPree, D., 16
DuRant, R. H., 50, 71
Dusenbury, L., 33

Earls, F., 70
Eastman, K. L., 3
Eckenrode, J., 11, 49, 69
Edwards, S., 64
Egami, Y., 43, 49
Egeland, B., 2, 15, 19, 23(n4), 44, 46, 50
Elder, G., 8, 51, 52
Elder, G. H., 2, 9, 15, 51, 76
Elliott, D. S., 71

SUBJECT INDEX

Abuse. *See* Maltreatment
Academic performance:
  age and, 13
  cross-domain effects and, 20
  ethnicity and, 31-32, 34, 36
  gender and, 11
  homelessness and, 67
  interventions for, 89-90
  parental functioning and, 45
  parenting behavior and, 47
  peers and, 64
  support networks and, 61, 62-63
  teenage mothers and, 26
  See also Educational outcomes; School
    experiences
Acculturation, 33
Adaptation:
  as a broad construct, 4
  diversity in, 1, 2
  See also Adjustment; Competence
Addiction. *See* Substance abuse
Adjustment:
  factors versus processes in, 2-3
  trajectories of, 18-21
  See also Adaptation; Competence
Adolescence:
  future enquiry into, 77, 78
  peers and, 65
  supportive parents and, 48-49
  See also Age differences; Teenage
    mothers; Teenage parents; Teenage
    pregnancy
Adulthood, and competence over time, 19
African American males, 33-34. *See also*
  Gender differences

African Americans:
  ethnicity comparisons for, 28-37
  families of, 28-37
  poverty rates of, 30
  relative risk for, 31-37
  socialization goals and, 28-30
Age differences, 12-13
  gender and, 8, 9, 10
  parenting behavior and, 25
Aggression:
  environment and, 71
  gender and, 8
  parenting behavior and, 47
  peers and, 17, 63-65, 80
  teenage mothers and, 26
Alcohol abuse. *See* Substance abuse
Alienation, 12
American Indians, 35
Anger, 8, 50
Anglos. *See* Caucasians
Anthropology, 79
Asian Americans, ethnicity comparisons for,
  28
Assessment of interventions, 91
Attributes, child, 7-23
Autonomy, 9, 10, 51

Beliefs, 61, 77. *See also* Values
Bicultural youth, 81
Biological processes, 82
Blacks. *See* African Americans
Blame, 17-18
Boys, 4, 27, 33-34. *See also* Gender
  differences
Bullying, 63. *See also* Aggression

ABOUT THE AUTHOR

Suniya S. Luthar is Associate Professor of Psychology and Education at Teachers College, Columbia University, and Director of Child & Family Research at the APT Foundation, New Haven. She received a Masters degree in Child Development from Delhi University, India, and a PhD in Developmental/Clinical Psychology from Yale University. Her interests are in developmental psychopathology and current studies involve adjustment processes among inner-city and suburban youth; vulnerability and resilience among substance abusers' children; and group psychotherapy for at-risk mothers. Professional honors include a dissertation award from the American Psychological Association's Division 37 and a Boyd McCandless Young Scientist Award from APA's Division 7.